A Year of Walks
in and around
The Wye Valley

Roy Woodcock

Published by Sigma Leisure – an imprint of
Sigma Press, 1 South Oak Lane, Wilmslow, Cheshire SK9 6AR, England.

British Library Cataloguing in Publication Data
A CIP record for this book is available from the British Library.

ISBN: 1-85058-744-2

Typesetting and Design by: Sigma Press, Wilmslow, Cheshire.

Cover photographs: Clockwise from top left – Dymock Woods; near Hay-on-Wye; May Hill; near Symonds Yat.

Maps and photographs: Roy Woodcock
Illustrations: Wendy Galassini

Printed by: MFP Design and Print

Disclaimer: the information in this book is given in good faith and is believed to be correct at the time of publication. No responsibility is accepted by either the author or publisher for errors or omissions, or for any loss or injury howsoever caused. Only you can judge your own fitness, competence and experience.

Preface

This series of circular walks visits 12 of the outstanding locations in the Wye Valley and crosses delightful countryside in all of them. The walks are not rugged or arduous, but more for walkers seeking fresh air and exercise, whilst seeing the entire length of the River Wye in all its moods throughout the year. The choice of walks is inevitably personal, looking for 12 interesting locations, and chosen to show the wide range of features of interest within the valley. Many famous honeypot locations are visited but it is also shown that even at busy weekends in summer it is possible to find quiet spots in this very popular tourist area.

Everywhere in the Wye Valley is scenically attractive and the middle and lower parts of the valley have been designated an AONB. More than 25 walks are included, with two or three options in each month. The walks range from 3 to 8 miles in length, but in most months it is possible to combine two of the walks to create a longer full day walk of from 8 – 12 miles, if required. The varied and variable length of walks is to enable walkers to have a leisurely half-day outing, or a walk to suit families with small children. There are always features of interest on the walks, whether it is a nature reserve with flowers or birds, an old church or abbey, the local geology, some local history or links with famous writers. Take your time and enjoy the walk, whatever the month. As Walter Hagen said in his comments on life: *You're only here for a short visit, so don't worry, don't hurry, and be sure you smell the flowers along the way.*

It is hoped that references to the weather, the landscape and the features of natural history that might be seen or experienced in each month will add to the interest and enjoyment of each walk. The features of natural history mentioned are generally those which are likely to be seen during the walk, not the rare or shy for which a lengthy wait may be required. It is hoped that the walks will enable you to discover features of the landscape which perhaps had not been noticed before, and to appreciate the countryside as it changes through the year. Each month has its own particular attractions, but although the walks specifically refer to a particular month, they can all be enjoyed at any time of the year. The maps and the detailed description of the route will enable anyone to follow these walks without danger of getting lost, although local maps may be useful in providing further information about the areas that are crossed. Any steep climbs are referred to in the description, as are locations for refreshment.

The weather comments included with each walk contain both the general or average for the month, but also specific to the region and to the particular year this was written. Countryside comments are also both specific and general, general to the month and the region, but with occasional more specific comments only relevant to the walk being described.

Advisory

Each walk is accompanied by a map and together with the detailed description of the walk this should enable anyone to find and follow the route. However it will be useful to have the 1:25,000 Pathfinder (or perhaps the 1:50,000 Landranger maps) in case of problems with the route and also to provide information and detail about the surrounding area. It is always advisable to carry a compass, which can be especially useful on bare hills, in woodlands or in fog, when sense of direction may be lost.

Many places will be muddy, especially in winter, and some sections of the walks are steep or stony. Therefore boots are advisable. It is also advisable, or even essential, to carry windproof and waterproof clothing, as well as a warm drink and some food if going out all day, even though there are locations for refreshment on most of the walks described.

Binoculars are very handy, especially if you are at all interested in bird life, and they sometimes help to pinpoint the location of stiles at the opposite side of large fields. Cameras too are useful, as all the walks contain many photogenic locations.

All details were correct at the time of walking (in 1999 or 2000). All the walks follow public rights of way, and were free from obstructions at the time when the routes described were last walked.

Beware of the winter possibility that the river will overflow its banks after periods of heavy rain or snow. Check with the local Tourist Information Centres if in doubt.

Contents

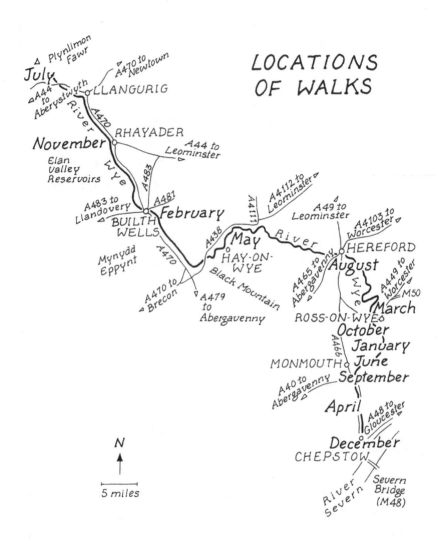

LOCATIONS
OF WALKS

△ Plynlimon Fawr

July

△A44 to Aberystwyth
Aberystwyth

△A470 to Newtown

LLANGURIG

River Wye

A470

RHAYADER

November

A44 to Leominster

Elan Valley Reservoirs

A483

A483 to Llandovery

A481

BUILTH WELLS

February

A4111

A4112 to Leominster

A49 to Leominster

A4103 to Worcester

River Wye

HEREFORD

Mynydd Eppynt

A470

A438

May

HAY-ON-WYE

A465 to Abergavenny

August

A449 to Worcester

M50

A470 to Brecon

A479 to Abergavenny

Black Mountain

ROSS-ON-WYE

March

October

January

MONMOUTH

A466

June

A40 to Abergavenny

September

April

A48 to Gloucester

December

N

CHEPSTOW

5 miles

River Severn

Severn Bridge (M48)

Introduction

*Once again
Do I behold these steep and lofty cliffs,
That on a wild secluded scene impress
Thoughts of more deep seclusion, and connect
The landscape with the quiet of the sky.*

These words of Wordsworth were written in 1798 after his visit to Llandogo when he had become an admirer of the Wye Valley scenery. He wrote of several other locations in the valley and there is a Wordsworth commemorative window in St George's church in Brinsop near where his brother-in-law lived.

Admired and appreciated by many since the time of Wordsworth, the river rises on Plynlimon, just 2 miles from the source of the Severn, and reaches the sea by joining the Severn Estuary just below Chepstow. On its course of about 135 miles, it flows through Powys (Montgomery, Radnor and Brecon) in a south-east and then southerly direction, before turning east to cross from Powys to Herefordshire at Hay-on-Wye, where the river forms the boundary for a few miles. It then turns to flow south, and for a short distance again forms a boundary, this time between Herefordshire and Gloucestershire near Symonds Yat. It then enters Monmouthshire (Gwent) and is the national boundary from Redbrook downstream, where the river continues to flow in a meandering but mainly southerly direction. It travels through a very rural environment, starting in fairly high hills of Mid Wales, yet passing through a series of market towns that have grown up along its banks, generally at bridging points.

The Wye Valley is noted for its wonderful scenery, and also for excellent walking. In addition to many miles of local footpaths there are several long-distance routes, too:

◆ The Marches Way extends the length of Wales, from Chester to Cardiff, passing close to Ludlow, and Hereford. Though not an official long-distance route and not waymarked, a guidebook is available.

◆ The Mortimer Trail is a 30-mile route from Ludlow to Kington, named after the Norman family of Mortimer, very large landowners in the border country. This path is clearly waymarked.

◆ Offa's Dyke Path is a National Trail, extending from Prestatyn to Chepstow, a total distance of 176 miles (285km), 67 miles of which are along the line of Offa's Dyke. Officially designated in 1967 and opened in 1971, it is a popular and challenging long-distance route with no huge hills to climb, but many short and steep slopes and a large number of stiles, which will test the fittest legs and knees. It is clearly waymarked and often closely follows the line of the earthwork built by King Offa (757-796) of Mercia in the 8th century, to denote the western boundary of Offa's Kingdom. It is close to the Wye at Chepstow, Monmouth and Hay. Several guidebooks are available.

◆ The Wye Valley Walk extends for 112 miles (181km) alongside the river or on the sides of the valley, from Rhayader to Chepstow, and is clearly signed, by arrows and the sign with the leaping salmon. Guidebooks are available. A 25-mile (40km) extension from Rhayader to Plynlimon is being planned.

◆ Wysis Way is a 55-mile long route which follows Offa's Dyke Path from Chepstow to Kymin before going eastwards across the northern Forest of Dean to May Hill, and then towards Gloucester and the Frome valley. It links the Wye, the Severn and the Thames.

◆ Gloucestershire Way links Offa's Dyke Path at Chepstow with the Severn Way at Gloucester, and also has links with the Cotswold Way, the Oxfordshire Way and the Heart of England Way. We pass an information board on May Hill (January Walk – see page 8) which mentions that the Gloucestershire Way provides a walk of 100 miles through the Forest of Dean, Severn Vale and the Cotswolds. It has a theme of Forest and Vale and High Blue Hill taken from the poem 'A Song of Gloucestershire' by Will Harvey of Minsterworth. F.W. Harvey, poet and musician, was born in Hartpury but brought up in Minsterworth, and was a great lover of Gloucestershire. He died 13th February 1957.

Information about these footpaths is available from the Tourist Information Centres and many local bookshops.

Area of Outstanding Natural Beauty

The Wye Valley was designated as an AONB in 1971. Stretching from Chepstow, to Mordiford just south of Hereford, it has a linear shape, with a total area of 326 sq.km (127 sq.ml.) The long and narrow shape includes areas of woodland, river bank, as well as limestone scenery with its special varieties of flora. Also, the banks of the river from the source to the mouth are classified as an SSSI (Site of Special Scientific Interest).

Geology and Landscape

The Upper Wye flows mostly through hilly country, largely on Silurian rocks, though the Plynlimon area is slightly older, of Ordovician age. Limestones and shales of the Silurian period can be seen in the anticline at Woolhope, very close to the route of the August walk. Silurian rocks also include sandstones as at Haugh Wood in the same area, and similar rocks form May Hill, which rises to nearly 1000ft (296m or 970ft). Silurian rocks give way to the Devonian (Old Red Sandstone) south and east of Builth Wells. The Caledonian orogenesis about 350 million years ago created land above sea level, and it was on this land that the Old Red Sandstone rocks were deposited, in desert conditions. Amongst the ORS deposits is the quartz conglomerate, to be seen on the walks in June and September.

The Middle Wye is mostly on the Old Red Sandstone of the Devonian period – where there are gentle meanders in a landscape of reddish soils, extending from Hereford through Monmouth to Tintern. The Wye is in a gentle phase, in contrast to its valley further upstream in the Welsh Hills, and downstream in the Tintern and Symonds Yat area. Even in this middle stretch of the river, water levels can be high and current powerful, and flooding does occur. The river is lined with fields, woods and orchards, and although a few old orchards survive, there are several newer younger orchards with small trees, easier for picking though not as popular with the rich variety of birds which inhabit the older orchards. In addition to the old trees in some orchards there are many areas of old woodland especially on the sloping ground and near the river bank, where they have never been cleared for farming.

In the Carboniferous period, which followed the Devonian, shallow seas and clear water covered the land, and dead sea creatures accumulated, to form limestones. The Lower Wye includes the famous Carboniferous limestone area of Symonds Yat, and the character of the valley changes quite dramatically at Goodrich. From Goodrich downstream, the river has Old Red Sandstone to the west, with Carboniferous Limestone a short distance to the east. The limestone, which contains many fossils notably crinoids and brachiopods, is found on both sides of the river from Tintern downstream to just beyond Chepstow.

The course of the Wye is complicated in this stretch of the valley, and south of Ross the river crosses and recrosses outcrops of Old Red Sandstone, Carboniferous Limestone and the rocks of the Coal Measure series, which are Carboniferous rocks younger than the Carboniferous Limestone. This all goes to show that the course of the Wye is not closely related to the present day scenery and geology, but has probably been established on the higher rocks of a landscape long since eroded.

This is known as superimposed drainage, meaning the pattern of the river has been imposed from above. This may have been caused by rejuvenation which occurs when a river gains renewed powers of erosion, possibly at the end of a glacial phase, when there are huge amounts of melt water available for extra erosive activity.

Best evidence of rejuvenation is in incised meanders, such as those deeply cut near Symonds Yat and downstream near Wintours Leap. As the river cut down to its new and lower level, erosion was too rapid for much lateral erosion to take place, and no new valley widening occurred, resulting in the meanders being deeply incised, as though cut into the rocks by a knife. There are occasional signs of old meanders being abandoned at a higher level as the river cut down to its new base level.

Outstanding evidence of such an abandoned meander is to be seen at Newland, visited in the September walks (page 109). Newland village is in a hanging valley, with the church on the edge, 122m (400ft) above the present day river. At Symonds Yat, the river is in an upland area, flows to lowland, and then immediately back into upland, having been formed sometime in the past, when the river was 400ft higher than at present.

Valley sides are often very steep especially in the areas of hard rocks, and although, as mentioned, the River Wye does not always follow structural lines, many variations in the valley slope can be related to structure and rock type. Where the rocks are dipping across the valley, one side is often steep and the other side is gentle. This is well seen near to Monmouth and Symonds Yat where there are also outcrops of the famous Quartz Conglomerate, a coarse sandstone rock containing smooth white pebbles of quartz. This rock formed as a beach deposit millions of years ago, and is generally harder than the adjacent rocks, standing up as a steep and near vertical slope on valley walls. Lumps of this rock have broken away in many places and can be seen on hillsides, and occasionally in the river, where they provide obstacles that add to the fun for canoeists

In the section of the river adjacent to the Forest of Dean there has been a long history of industrial development, some of which can be seen, or imagined, in the Tintern and Chepstow walks. The industrial centres used local coal, iron and timber, as well as making use of the river as a routeway – especially upstream as far as Brockweir (see April walk, page 56).

The limestone cliffs and outcrops, with their rich wealth of trees and plants on both sides of the river extend from below Tintern to Chepstow and beyond. It is only as the Severn Estuary comes into sight below Chepstow that the younger Triassic rocks are to be found – as seen in the December walk to Sedbury (see page 153).

History

Earliest inhabitants in the Wye Valley include cave dwellers near to Symonds Yat, and there were many people as well as many tribal battles in the Wye Valley before the time of the Romans. They built major settlements in South Wales most notably at Caerwent, and in the Wye Valley there were large Roman settlements near Weston-Under-Penyard and also Magnis near Hereford. After the Romans, during the Dark Ages, the Welsh people (the Ancient Brits) fought to keep out the new Anglo Saxon invaders. Not until the time of King Offa was the line of the Welsh boundary created.

After the arrival of William the Conqueror, it was the Normans who worked hard to establish a boundary, and to help achieve this, several castles were built, including those near the River Wye at Chepstow, Monmouth, Goodrich, where the river flows close to the English-Welsh border. In later times, it was Edward I who really conquered Wales and brought some stability to the area which enabled agriculture to develop and prosperity to increase.

This lovely river is even more popular now than it was in the past, though it has been attracting visitors for more than 200 years. In the 18th century poets, artists and the wealthy upper classes regarded the Wye Tour as a socially desirable activity. William Gilpin wrote a detailed guidebook 'Observations on the River Wye and several points in South Wales' in 1782 (based on his tour or 1770), but there are many guidebooks now, including this one! Wordsworth was one of several famous visitors, having stayed at Llandogo in 1798.

The Wye is still noted as a beautiful valley with a clean river, and this has obviously been a great help to fish. Salmon were famous, and numerous, in the past, but by the 1860s they had become scarce because of overfishing and industrialisation (building of weirs made it much easier to catch fish). There have been improvements in stocks this century, and there are also coarse fish, a few lampreys and many eels and elvers. Fishing is a good source of income now, and day tickets are available in several locations along the river, notably at Ross, near Hereford and at Hay.

The river as well as the valley has been an important routeway serving local industry, especially connected with the minerals and timber of the Forest of Dean. In spite of tides, shallows and floods, the river was an important routeway, until the arrival of the railways in the 1870s. Industrial growth in the valley was helped by water power from fast flowing tributary streams. In the 18th and 19th centuries a few trows (similar to those on the Severn) sailed from Chepstow to Brockweir, which was the tidal limit. Cargoes were there transferred to barges which continued upstream as far as Ross and Hereford – the flat-bottomed barges could carry up to about 60 tonnes of cargo. Now the river is just used for pleasure, with cruising, canoeing, rafting, fishing and walking. Note the names of river-side pubs such as the Boat Inn at Redbrook or Anchor Inn at Ross, formerly connected with river traffic, but now more linked with modern tourism.

Natural History

The Wye Valley is a wonderful location for wild life, with water birds on the river and a variety of other birds in the woodlands on the valley sides, notably pied flycatchers and wood warblers in the summer. In the upper course the hill country supports dipper and grey wagtail on the rivers and kites and buzzards in the surroundings. There are now a few otters back on the Wye, and some less welcome mink. Rabbits are very numerous in the fields and woodlands, much appreciated by the foxes, buzzards – and those that get killed on the roads are a source of food for magpies and crows. The Carboniferous limestone areas have their own special flora, and the steep slopes have enabled flowers and old woodlands to survive. A few of the steep limestone slopes provide safe haven as nesting sites for jackdaws, crows and even peregrine falcon.

As mentioned in the January, March and August Walks (pages 8, 35 and 97), orchards are still important in the Lower Wye Valley, especially in Herefordshire.

January
May Hill area and Dymock

Both of this month's walks are close to Newent, on the margins of the Wye Valley. The May Hill walk keeps well away from floods in the valley, climbing to the top of the famous landmark and viewpoint and then circling through the woods and the common land which surround the hill. The second walk crosses farmland to follow a circuit near Dymock to pass several of the locations related to the famous group of poets who lived in this area at the beginning of World War I. The land can be very wet and muddy, especially in the woods, unless frozen by low temperatures. My last visit to May Hill was a glorious sunny day early in 2000, when the overnight frost was slow to clear, and just beneath the surface on May Hill the ground was still frozen, similar to the permafrost of the Arctic Tundra of northern Canada. On a clear day the famous and distinctive clump of trees can be seen from miles around, including the Malvern Hills and M5. In reverse of course, all these locations can be seen from the top of the hill, with its 360-degree views.

Lengths of walks: May Hill – 6 miles, taking about 3 hours. The Dymock walk is about 10 miles (with a short cut of 6), requiring 4-5 hours (or 3 hours).

Terrain: gently undulating around Dymock, but there is a climb up to the top of May Hill – very warming for a January day though the summit is exposed and can be very windy.

Maps: O.S. Outdoor Leisure 14, the Wye Valley and Forest of Dean, for May Hill; Explorers 190 (formerly number 14), Malvern Hills and 189, Hereford and Ross-on-Wye for Dymock. O.S. Landrangers 149 and 162 cover this area.

Starting points: for May Hill, use the parking space alongside the narrow road which runs round the north-western side of the hill GR692223, reached either from the A40 or along narrow roads from Newent, passing the National Birds of Prey Centre and Clifford's Mesne. For the Poets' Walk, start in Dymock near the church GR701312 or at Preston church GR680346.

Public Transport: bus services run to Newent and Dymock, and along the A40 a mile to the south of May Hill. Occasional buses run from Ledbury to Ross via Glasshouses.

Facilities: nearest town is Ross-on-Wye, which has a choice of refreshments and a Tourist Information Centre (phone 01989 562768). Newent also has a Tourist Information Centre (phone 01531 822468).

Weather

January is generally a mixture of cold bursts and mild spells, though three out of four are mostly mild. The last really cold January was 1987, and 1999 proved to be one of the typical mild months, with an average temperature of 5°C, well above the long-term average of 2.9°C. Daily maxima in the Wye Valley were often in the 9-13°C range, with up to 15°C being recorded. There was a slightly cooler spell from 7th-9th, with north-westerly winds and near the end of the month were a few dry days associated with northerly weather. This was particularly useful as the month was generally very wet and flooding was widespread. Much of the month was dominated by un-settled low pressure with weather coming from the Atlantic where the water was warmer than average. Gales were frequent, especially in the north-west and it proved to be the wettest January for 30 years in many localities, especially in Wales, Welsh Borders and western England. Many of the weather systems were fast moving, giving very changeable conditions, and surprisingly, in spite of heavy rainfall, sunshine totals were well up to average.

The Countryside

In such a wet month with widespread flooding, it was decided to take a walk on higher ground of the valley margin rather than down near the river. May Hill was chosen for its fine views on the exposed hill top, with sheltered conditions in the surrounding woodlands, to give the best of wintry walking conditions. The countryside looked very orderly, with mostly shorn hedges, and silhouettes of bare trees, some of which (e.g. willows) were knee-deep in water. It is worth while looking at the shapes of trees in their bare condition, and noting the differences in tree bark. Parts of the countryside were looking surprisingly green, with many fields of grass, still contain-ing a little nutrient for sheep and beef cattle wintering out in the fields. This is a pastoral area, with many horses too, but a few fields are arable, with clingy mud, through which crops are already show-ing an inch or two of growth. Birds to be seen include a few lap-wings, as well as fieldfares, redwings, finches and gulls.

In "La Belle Dame Sans Merci", Keats wrote:

> *The sedge is withered from the lake,*
> *And no birds sing.*

In spite of this, there are a few birds singing, with just an occasional burst – robin, wren, great tit, nuthatch, and even a thrush or blackbird occasionally especially nearer the end of the month. More birds were heard singing this year than is usual, and blackbirds have been heard singing especially in towns, perhaps because of extra warmth, light or shelter. They tend to sing just in the afternoons at first, although later in the year, a better and fuller song will be heard at all hours of the day. My **bird of the month** is the buzzard, often seen floating above, sitting on the fence posts or

Buzzard

walking in the fields searching for earthworms or beetles. They also eat carrion, and rabbits if they can catch them. They generally nest in trees, and spend much of their time merely sitting in trees. Whilst floating overhead, often being harassed by crows, they may be looking for possible food sources, but most of their hunting is done from perches. They have been most numerous in the hilly parts of Britain especially in the west, but have been steadily increasing in recent years, and extending their range – an ornithological success story.

May Hill

Though only 296m (970ft) in height, this is a prominent landmark nonetheless. The summit trees resemble a Mohican hairstyle when seen from a distance, and include Corsican pines, planted in 1888 to celebrate Queen Victoria's golden jubilee (1887). More trees were added to celebrate Queen Elizabeth's silver jubilee, and still more for the Queen Mother's 80th birthday. So this cap of trees is meant to be long lasting, as replacements for the future are already growing.

Ivor Gurney wrote :

> _May Hill that Gloucester dwellers_
> _'Gainst every sunset see_

Another local poet, John Masefield was also moved to write about May Hill, in his 'Everlasting Mercy'.

> _Above the plains of Gloucester,_
> _She lifts her rounded head._

In the same poem he wrote:

> _For all the hills in Gloucestershire, MAY she is the queen._

Much of May Hill Common is owned by the National Trust, but the summit is 4 acres (1.6 ha.) of SSSI managed by the parish. There must have been a small camp up here, but there are no real remains, only a shallow ditch. An old custom was for local people to have a mock battle on May Day, to start the summer, in which the two sides represented summer and winter. Summer always won!

Newent

This ancient market town contains several timber framed houses in addition to the fine Market House which dates from the 16th or 17th century, though restored in 1864. Parts of St Mary church are from the 13th and 14th centuries, and lead from the roof was used by Royalists to make bullets in the Civil War. The roof subsequently collapsed in 1674, destroying the nave, which was rebuilt later in the 17th century. An old court house next to the church and the interesting museum of Victorian Life is in the Shambles (not open through the winter – phone 01531 822144).

National Birds of Prey Centre

Located near Newent, this was founded in 1967 as a Falconry Centre, and has become one of the world's largest collections of birds of prey, with more than 200 birds. There is a coffee shop, gift shop, picnic area and a large car park. It is open February to November, 7 days a week (phone 01531 820286).

Dymock

This small village grew on the site of an ancient settlement dating back to Roman times. It has a garage, a post office and several new houses, not far from the old pub the Beauchamp Arms which is located adjacent to the Norman church of St Mary the Virgin. The church's sculptured doorway with tympanum depicting the Tree of life is the work of the Dymock School of Sculpture (also to be seen at Kempley – see March walk, page 39). Amongst the interesting features in the interior are modern glass by Kempe and a small exhibition for the Dymock Poets. The village has given its name to a group of poets who lived or visited here in the years just before World War I. Lascelles Abercrombie was the first, having moved here in 1911 and was joined by others in 1913 and 1914. Abercrombie lived at The Gallows in nearby Ryton, and Rupert Brooke and John Drinkwater stayed there for several months in 1913, then Robert Frost and family stayed there for a few months in 1914-15. Wilfrid Wilson Gibson lived at the Old Nail Shop and it was he and Abercrombie who produced a Quarterly Magazine called *New Numbers* from 1914-1915, and in the last issue were the famous lines by Rupert Brooke, in his poem 'The Soldier'.

> *If *I should die think only this of me*
> *That there's a corner of a foreign field*
> *That is forever England.*

Rupert Brooke and Edward Thomas both died in the Great War.

Dymock is also noted as the centre of a wild daffodil growing area, and though not in flower in January, many of the plants will be growing before the end of this month (see March walk, page 38).

The May Hill walk

From the car parking place (1), cross the road and walk up the grassy slope between silver birch trees and bracken. As we climb, the already distant views become even greater and reveal more hills over to the west beyond Ross-on-Wye and the Wye Valley. Looking back over the car parking space can be seen several church spires and towers, not only in Ross and Weston-under-Penyard (see the September walk – page 126) but also in Linton and Aston Ingham. On this steady climb there may be horses, which graze on the common. Reach a wooden kissing gate in a stone wall beyond which is the open grassy climb to the clump of trees on the top of the hill. Views now open up to the left (east) and then straight ahead towards the Severn Estuary. Over to the right can be seen the mast on the hill near Cinderford.

The famous clump of trees has smaller younger conifers in an outer fringe, with the taller and older pines beyond. Seats are available, space for picnics and in the middle of the trees the two plaques, one for the younger trees planted by Longhope Parish Council and were replenished in Jubilee Year of 1977, and the other for Queen Victoria's Golden Jubilee.

Our onward route goes straight ahead, following the Gloucestershire Way (see Introduction, page 2) which has come up to this hill top along a path from the right (as we approach the clump). Walk from the triangulation point across small remnants of

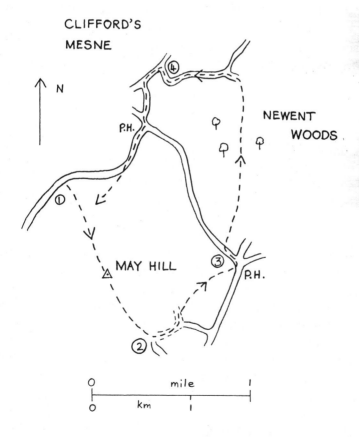

circular mounds, and descend gently to come alongside a wood on our left, with a line of beech bordering the larch trees. Reach a gate with Wysis Way and Gloucestershire Way signs and go straight ahead, still descending, in the edge of the trees, with an open field to the right.

Reach a house on the left and a junction of paths and tracks, where we go straight ahead, along the Gloucestershire Way, but after about 100 metres, fork left off this path **(2)**. Follow a yellow arrow along a muddy track going slightly downhill, passing a house on the left (with a lot of glass) and reach a driveway, where we turn left, following a public footpath sign. After a few metres, go over the stile by a large gate, on to a broad track, but after 20 metres fork right off this track, to go downhill (No Horses sign) following a footpath that is part of the Wysis Way, linking the Offa's Dyke Path to the Thames Way.

Descend quite steeply at first, and then more gently, through an area of mixed woodland, rich in wild flowers (including bluebells and wood sorrel) and bird song in the spring. Muddy patches are likely, or inevitable if the ground is not frozen, and as we find the track becoming very muddy, look for a small and drier path just a few metres to the right. Move on to this alternative route which stays nearly parallel with the main track, and soon enters a wonderful grove of tall redwood trees, where there are also many small trees, the result of self reseeding. Here there are likely to be tits and goldcrests busy in their search for food in mid-winter. Rejoin the main path again, walk on down to a stile by the gate, and the road. Our onward route is to the left along this narrow road, but a few metres to the right is the temptation of the Glasshouse Inn, where drinks and food are available if required **(3)**.

The Glasshouse Inn takes its name from the Huguenot refugees who set up a glass furnace in 1598, using fuel from the Newent Woods, and water from the stream flowing beneath the road, between the stile and the Glasshouse Inn. The glassmakers depended on Newent Woods as a source of charcoal, but the industry declined when coal became available in other locations.

Walk along the road for about 200 metres, and in the field to the right was the location of the old glassworks, and beyond is the castellated Clifford Manor. Go right, over the stile and head diagonally

Clifford Manor, near Glasshouse

left through the field to a stile leading into the woods. At first the woods are quite open and rich in spring flowers (wood anemones, daffodils, bluebells), but as the path gets deeper into these old woods, denser growth will be found with many fallen trees but also large numbers of young trees. Last year's leaves line the path, which is narrow but quite clear, and heads in a northerly direction, soon to reach a major cross track beyond which is a dark coniferous area. Turn left along this track, cross over the small stream and follow the track as it bends right, and is soon back on the more or less northerly direction. Stay on this track and when it reaches a bigger and gravelled cross track, keep straight ahead on a footpath in a more open patch of mixed woodland, including some larch. Join on to a track, which leads us past a small car park for fishermen and along the right side of Huntley Pool.

Keep straight on beyond this lake into an area of recent planting, and when the track splits take the right fork, and after 100 metres, as it splits again, take the left fork, still heading northwards, and with deciduous trees on the right, but coniferous to the left. Pass a few buildings visible to the right, and at a track turn left to pass Woodgate Farm and reach a narrow road. Keep straight ahead along this road for half a mile, to Clifford's Mesne **(4)**.

Just past the first houses, as the road bends right, notice the tracks going left, and the first of the signs 'Road used as a Public Path' – here are several in and around the village. As the road climbs slightly, do not be fooled by the model heron in the pool on the left just through the hedge, and at the T-junction turn left towards Glasshouse. Pass the newish house on the right, in the old quarry, whose outcrop can be seen behind the house, and St Peter's church; this stone building dates from the 13th century but was restored in the 1880s.

Fork left at the junction, by the phone box following the sign to Glasshouse 1¼ miles, and pass to the left of the village hall. Start to climb and turn right to go up steeply past the Yew Tree Inn (01531 820719). Beyond the pub we reach a cattle grid and the beginning of May Hill Common, with its National Trust sign. Where a path goes off to the left, signposted to May Hill, follow this as it climbs steadily through the silver birch and bracken, as far as a gate and stone wall, where we turn right to return to the starting point.

The Dymock Walk

This 10-mile walk crosses the area loved by the Dymock Poets. This was the name given to a group of poets who lived in this area for a few years, from 1911-1916, and were visited by other poets, who came to enjoy the beautiful and inspirational scenery and company. There are two Poets Path Walks, and we are taking in part of Poets' Path I and more of Poets' Path II as we explore the surrounding area where they lived and walked.

Start from the Beauchamp Inn **(1)** and walk via Wintours Green to pass the left side of the church. Leave the churchyard via an iron kissing gate and head diagonally right across the field to a stile by a gate, and then out on to the road. Turn left and walk over the bridge and after a further 100 metres, reach a stile where we turn right. Cross the middle of the field, noting the small River Leadon on the right, which occasionally floods up into this field. Go over another stile to cross the next field and one more stile and field, heading towards a lone house. We reach a few steps down to a narrow road, and keep straight ahead to pass the houses we had been walking towards, Elmbridge Villas. So far, we have been on the route of Poets' Path I, but we now join Poets Path II on which we remain for the rest of this walk.

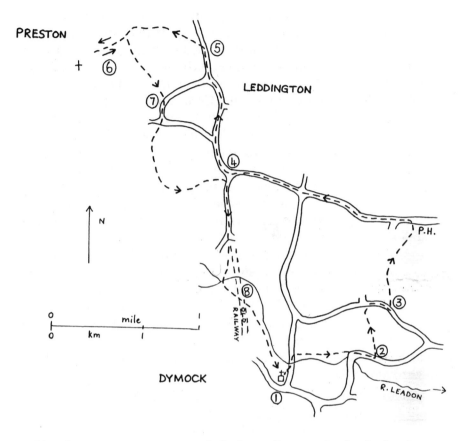

PRESTON

LEDDINGTON

DYMOCK

R. LEADON →

After about 200 metres, turn left through a gap in the hedge by an
iron gate **(2)**, and go slightly left of straight ahead across the middle
of the field, heading towards a white house (The Burtons) in the distance. There were formerly two fields in this next stretch of the walk,
but many hedges have been removed to enable farmers to use bigger
machines to reduce costs and improve productivity. The landscape
is much more open than in the days of the Dymock Poets. Robert
Frost wrote that:

> *"The fields are so small and the trees so numerous along the
> hedges that, as my friend Thomas says in the loveliest book on
> spring in England, you may think for a little distance that the
> country was solid woods."*

Go slightly uphill and diverging from the hedge to our right, to reach a footbridge with small V stiles at each end. Cross the bridge and turn right to walk alongside the hedge, looking out for a large alder tree, probably with cones and catkins at this time of year. Continue gradually uphill to reach a stile and the road where we turn right. Ignore the left turn to Broom's Green and The Burtons, but we keep straight ahead, and after about 100 metres over the hedge to our right is a small pond, remnants of a moat. After a further 100 metres, where the road bends right, we go left **(3)** a few metres along a drive and then over a stile to head straight out across the field towards a hedge visible on the other side. At this hedge is a stiled footbridge and we continue ahead, with the hedge on our left. Follow the hedge to the end of this field, ignoring a stile with a path going left. There is also a ditch to our left lined with hazel trees possibly laden with catkins. At the end of the field go over the stile, and a quick left-right past a pond, but still straight ahead really following the edge of the field, now a wire fence. Just past a small wood of young trees, our path goes left through a few trees and over two stiles to continue along the field boundary. At the end of the next field are twin stiles where a new hedge has been planted and straight-ahead across the next field leads to a stiled footbridge and then a narrow path taking us through to the road.

About 100 metres to the right is The Horseshoe Inn, if refreshment is required, but our onward route is to the left. We pass the Broom's Green, Donnington and Ryton Village Hall by a left turn but just keep straight ahead. The left turn is signposted to Knight's Green and Ryton, and Ryton is the location of the house where Lascelles Abercombie lived but nothing remains of the house now, apart from a few brick steps. Close to the site of the house, is part of the wood that gave the inspiration for Abercrombie's poem about Ryton Firs.

We keep straight ahead along the road for more than half a mile, to reach the crossroads at Greenway. But before reaching there, pass a line of fine Scots pine where, to the right, there are good views to Donnington Hall with Ledbury church spire beyond, in the distance. At the crossroads is The Old Nail Shop where Wilfrid Wilson Gibson lived with his wife from 1913-17. Keep straight ahead along the road signposted to Much Marcle, and soon pass over the River Leadon, lined with trees – look out for a kingfisher. Reach the line of the old railway, from Ledbury to Gloucester and as we climb slightly up to the humpback bridge, note a large swollen ash tree down to our right with a few clumps of snowdrops around it. Once over the railway walk on to pass Drew's farm on the left, and Greenway House on the right, with its small pond and remnants of a moat (4).

At the T-junction the onward way is to the right to complete a 4 mile circuit back to this point – coming through the gate opposite, but for a **Short Cut** back to Dymock turn left here following the signpost to Dymock and Much Marcle.

Short Cut

Drew's Farm is on the left, and one of a few orchards in this locality can be seen over the hedge. Follow this road for about 600 metres and when the road bends right, and a track goes left to pass over an old railway bridge, we turn left along this track for about 30 metres and then go right over a stile into a large field. There are buildings to the left of this field, but the official route goes out into the middle of the field towards the telegraph pole and the overhead wire. Pass a lone tree and aim for the far end of the field where the three larger electricity wires on twin posts cross over the river. Near the end of the field on the left margin, can be seen the old railway embankment built to allow the line to cross the flat flood plain. We cross the stream at a farm bridge – Monks Bridge – and go over a stile and cross a small field to a stile in a hedge, with the electricity wires almost overhead. These wires turn away to the right, but we go sharp left towards the hedge at the far-left side of the field. Cross over the stile by an iron gate, then the route of the old railway and another stile (8).

Turn right here, alongside but not quite parallel to the old railway line, heading towards a stile in the hedge ahead. Keep straight ahead across the middle of next field to a stile to the left of a pollarded tree, and across the next field and come alongside the River Leadon. Go over another stile, cross a narrow field, with farm buildings up to the right, and over another stile where the path turns right to follow the river, which has a few wonderful meanders. These have text book characteristics, with the steep eroded slope on the outside of the bend and deposition and flat land on the inside of the bend, where willow trees are growing. Cross a footbridge and stile to get into the next field, which is quite small, then head slightly left to the far corner to a stiled footbridge to get into the final field of this walk. On our right is some new building, as we climb up the slope to the kissing gate leading us back into the churchyard.

Main Walk

Turn right along the road following the signpost to Leddington. On our right is a small orchard, possibly with sheep grazing beneath the trees and on the left is one of several large fields seen on this walk. Along this narrow road to Leddington, we pass a turning to the left and then a private road to the right, to Upham. Cuckoo pint is sprouting in the hedge bottoms and there are likely to be a variety of finches along the trimmed hedges around here. The next few buildings make up Leddington, and on the right just before a bend in the road is the entrance to Mirabels Farm with an old grindstone and a few clumps of snowdrops. The road bends left and then right, and we keep ahead along the road towards Ledbury. Descend to a small hollow to pass a gate and footpath sign going left, which is our route, but first continue for about 200 metres to look at Little Iddens, which was rented by Robert Frost in 1914, and Glyn Iddens where Eleanor Farjeon (who wrote the hymn 'Morning has Broken') stayed in August 1914. It was in June 1914 that Robert Frost wrote about Little Iddens:

"When we first came, the meadows were covered with yellow daffodils and the cuckoo had just begun to sing. For nearly two months it sang all day."

Retrace steps to continue our walk, over the gate on the left mentioned previously **(5)**, and head diagonally right across the corner of the field to a stile, and through a small paddock to another stile. Go straight ahead across the field, descending to a few steps, a plank footbridge over a stream and then a stile. Keep straight ahead, uphill, passing the telegraph pole and a lone tree in the middle of the field. The path leads on to the far corner of this field, just to the right of the attractive house, known as Oldfields and having links with Edward Thomas who rented rooms here in 1914. At the end of the field go over a stile, and keep straight ahead across a small field to the corner of the hedge ahead.

Climb over the stile and walk alongside the hedge on the right,

Oldfields

until it begins to bend right. At this point head slightly left and walk on aiming towards the large barn and the black and white of Preston Court seen ahead. At the end of the field, turn left to follow the boundary fence alongside the stream, to reach a stiled footbridge. Turn right here and go straight across two fields, and stiles to reach Preston Court and the church of St John the Baptist, where John Masefield was christened. He used this location as the basis for a scene in his poem "Reynard the Fox", although he changed the name to Tineton. Preston House is a timber framed house from the early 17th century, with fine diagonal brick chimneys **(6)**.

After a look round Preston, walk away from the church and the Court to retrace steps across the two fields to return to the stiled footbridge over the stream Ludstock Brook. Turn right, downstream, but diverge to the left away from the stream, heading diagonally uphill, towards a lone tree on the top of the slope. May Hill comes into sight, and about 30 metres to the left of an iron gate and cattle trough is our stile in the corner of the field. Once over this, follow the hedge on the left as far as a stile and go over here and turn right. Head diagonally down to the right, diverging from the hedge to reach a stiled footbridge at the bottom of the slope. Go straight ahead, well away from the buildings ahead to our left, towards a lone tree peeping over the brow of the hill. Near the tree is a stile and we go over on to a narrow lane, and turn right **(7)**.

Pass a small orchard on our right, before reaching a T-junction where we go ahead through a gate and diagonally left for a few

Preston House

metres to a stiled footbridge. Once over this turn right to follow the hedge to the end of this field, where we turn left. The buildings of New House are over to our right. Follow the hedge and, after nearly 100 metres, do a right then left kink, and continue ahead with the hedge on the left, to a stile at the end of this field. When last walking along here, I heard skylarks singing.

Cross straight over the narrow section of the next field, with the large barns of Rosehill over to the right, to walk alongside the hedge on the right, to another stile. Once over this, turn left to follow the hedge on the left. The footpath should diverge slightly away from the hedge but heading to the far side of a large field and a gate. Through the gate, the path heads diagonally left across the middle of the next large field, to a gateway gap in the hedge visible at the top of the slope. From this gate follow the line of the hedge on our left and walk alongside another large field, with the large barns of Drew's Farm ahead and the wooded hills near Ledbury ahead to the left, with the profile of the British Camp on the Herefordshire Beacon peeping through one of the gaps. We reach a gate and the T-junction **(4)** we passed about 2 hours ago, and turn right here along the road, following the signpost to Dymock and Much Marcle, as described in the Short Cut above.

February
Builth Wells

Two short walks which can be joined together if desired, each of which climbs from the sheltered valley up on to the exposed hills near the distinctive Aberedw Rocks.

Lengths of walks: the Aberedw walk is just over 5 miles and could be completed in 3 hours – a good walk after an excellent lunch at the village pub. The walk from the old station at Erwood is also about 5 miles.

Terrain: in each walk there is a lengthy but not very steep climb, followed by a more gentle stretch on the plateau and ending with a steady descent. In winter, the exposed plateau surface can be very bleak, and appropriate clothing and food and warm drinks should be taken by anyone following this walk. A compass ought to be carried in case the cloud level descends to restrict visibility.

Maps: O.S. Landranger 147 Elan Valley and Builth Wells/Cwm Elan a Llanfair-ym-Muallt; Explorer 188 Builth Wells /Llanfair-ym-Muallt.

Starting points: in Aberedw, GR079473. Also, there is parking at the Old Railway station at the Erwood Craft Centre, GR 089439

Public Transport: buses run along the A470 to Builth Wells, and the Swansea to Shrewsbury railway line passes through Builth. Nearest TIC is in Builth Wells (telephone 01982 553307) and Builth has a wide choice of refreshments

Facilities: there is a pub at Aberedw, and a small café at the Craft Centre at Erwood (01982 560674 – open mid-February to December). Parking is available along the side of the road in the village of Aberedw, or perhaps at the pub, with permission, if you are having a meal there. The food is highly recommended.

Weather

Generally a cold month, and often the coldest of the year, but this year (1999) saw an alternation of mild and cold spells, except in northern Scotland where cold spells were prolonged. The mild spells were in the majority and the temperatures for the month were above average because of south-westerly winds, and the Central England Average Temperature was 5.3°C., compared with the long term (30 year) average of 3.6°C. Temperatures of 14-15°C. were recorded in mid-month. High pressure to the north brought winds round to the north-west to give several short bursts of Arctic weather with frosts and some snow flurries, but there was no easterly weather. The presence of high pressure for part of the month helped to give a dry month, and so the floods of January were able to fully subside. The old saying:

February brings the rain, and thaws the frozen lakes again was hardly appropriate this year. More relevant perhaps was the comment about cold winds from the north written by Charles Kingsley in his 'Ode to the North East Wind' –

'Tis hard grey weather, Breeds hard English men.

The Countryside

Several mild days and days with sunshine gave a spring like feeling to much of the month, even though frosts and snow were seen. On the milder or sunny days, bird song increased, and by mid-month chasing and fluttering was seen in many species. Birds, like many plants get the feeling it is spring, even when temperatures are too low for humans to be convinced.

If February brings no rain, 'tis neither good for grass nor grain.

Even if grass and grain are slow to grow early in the year, they can generally catch up as the weather improves. This certainly was a dry month, and the floods of January had subsided, but the ground remained very wet, as is inevitable in February with no evaporation and the accumulation of water through December and January. Grazing animals were back in the fields, including the riverside meadows (hams). In the lowlands, the first lambs had appeared and crops in the arable fields were showing slight signs of growth. This is also the month for harvesting some of the winter vegetables such as swedes. This horrible task seems to have to cope with either frost or mud, as was well portrayed in the film version of 'Tess of the d'Urbevilles'. Grass certainly grew during the month, and many of the wild flowers were at the best, with the snowdrops prolific in many places. Tradition has it that they will be in flower by Candlemas Day (2nd February), and this was certainly true this year. There were even a few early daffodils, and pussy willows on some of the riverside trees. By the end of the month, the first few hawthorn shoots were out too, on many of the hedgerows. Moles had been moving around, when the ground was soft, as their food, the worms, were moving back up to the surface. As the moles make new tunnels, they push up their hills of fine soil. Bird song always increases, especially during mild spells such as from the 17th-20th, and the courting and displaying began. The countryside tradition was that this all began on St Valentine's Day, as described by Chaucer. St Valentine's Day, the 14th February, has no connection with St Valentine, but was derived from the Lupercalia, a Roman fertility feast. Pigeons are already breeding – and rooks are visiting their nests again. The dipper, my **bird of the month**, will also begin to breed, as they are very early to build their nest, often behind a waterfall. This unique bird, looking like a large black and white wren has unwebbed feet, but can swim, and it dives to the bed of the stream to search for food. It walks on the bed, turning over small rocks in the search for insects and larvae. They are a welcome sight on any river, as they are an indication of clean water. They do not thrive if water is too acid or polluted, because there are no insects for food. They are most usually seen flying at speed low across the water, or perched on a rock, bobbing and curtseying. Up on the hills around the Aberedw rocks, nature is a long way behind the conditions in the valleys. Sheep will be grazing but with no lambs as yet, and summer visitor birds have not yet arrived.

Dipper

Builth Wells

This market town, with its weekly market on Mondays, is situated at a crossing point of the Wye with an ornate 18th-century bridge, and also at the confluence of the Irfon with the Wye. On the site of this ancient settlement, there is evidence of the Romans and also the Danes, who razed the town in AD 893. There are still remains of an 11th-century Norman motte and bailey castle, of which only the earthworks remain. The castle was rebuilt in the 13th century, on the order of Edward I, and the church of St Mary also dates from that century, though largely rebuilt in 1870. Much of the town was destroyed by fire in 1691 and few buildings remain from earlier times. The main growth was as a spa town in the 18th century when mineral springs were found at Park Wells (a mile north-west of the town centre), but now is more famous and important as the site of the Royal Welsh Show in late July. The mid-Wales railway used to go from Builth to Rhayader, but there is still the railway link from Builth Road station to Shrewsbury. Overlooking Builth are the quarries at Llanelwedd, a source of volcanic rocks used for local buildings but also providing stone for use in building the dams in the Elan Valley. Builth is an important tourist centre and is a popular location for fishing throughout the year.

The well-known poem 'The Wye' by Donald Hughes says:

> *The Wye at Rhayader races along*
> *By Builth it is still but a talkative song*
> *Through Hay and through Hereford onward it goes,*
> *And it grows,*
> *As it flows.*

Aberedw

The famous Aberedw rocks are of Silurian shale and stand 185 metres (600ft) above the Wye, and also above the smaller River Edw on which stands the village. The Edw gorge was probably formed after the Ice Age when a lake full of melt water was able to carve an outlet through the Aberedw rocks. Aberedw has a castle, important in the struggle to retain independence from England, but only small remains are to be seen, due to the passage of the centuries and also the building of the Mid Wales Railway in 1864 which cut through the site.

Llywelyn

Also sometimes spelled Llewellyn or Llewelyn, he was described as the last Welsh Prince, or was he also really the first, because there had been no thought of a united country until that time. History or legend suggests that Llywelyn the Last hid in a cave in the Aberedw rocks up above his castle in Aberedw, whilst hiding from the English – the local people in Builth had not been willing to hide him. He had been campaigning near here in December 1282, but was caught and killed near Cilmery to the west of Builth, where there is now a Memorial Stone. The cave is to the left of our path on the descent from the rocks towards Aberedw, but is not on a right of way. It may possibly have been used by St Cewydd in the 5th century.

Aberedw Rocks

The walk from Aberedw

Start at the Seven Stars **(1)** and walk past the church, named after the 6th-century St Cewydd, the brother of Gildas. Note the porch built from huge oak logs. Walk down the hill, between a few houses in very good repair, many with crowds of snowdrops. The River Edw is to the right, and on the rocks in the middle of this tumbling stream, you may be lucky enough to catch sight of a dipper bobbing up and down. The road splits by a telephone box and we fork right, with the river still to our right and a wooded slope rich in bird life. On a mild day, bird song will include the robin and thrush.

Cross the river over the stone bridge, beyond which the road splits **(2)** and we take the right fork passing the No Through Road sign. This is a sunken lane between banks and hedges for a time as we climb, and then emerge into more open views, still with grassy fields alongside the narrow road. Pass beneath the electricity wires, and where the surfaced road ends a track goes left to a farm, but we keep straight ahead along the muddy and stony track, still climbing. The track begins to bend left, and reaches a gate beyond which is open hillside.

About 30 metres beyond the gate, near a meeting point of several tracks, we turn sharp right to go diagonally up the hillside on a grassy track through bracken. Some gorse will also be seen as we climb and a few rocks outcrop on the track, as we begin to bend slightly to the left. The steepness decreases, and we reach a cross tracks but keep straight ahead. The climb becomes more gradual as we approach the line of electricity wires again, but then bends slightly left away from the wires, as we reach the flattish plateau area. Good views open up all around, with larger prominent hills away to the south and south-east towards Hay-on-Wye and the Black Hills, and the smaller Llandeilo Hill away to our left, north-east. Just beyond an old Boundary Stone we reach a major cross tracks **(3)** , where we turn right, to walk beneath the electricity wires, with a pylon just to the right of our path.

A clear grassy track leads us south-west across the plateau through the bracken, with a little gorse and bilberry plants, and a small lake (by old quarry) over to the left. The track bends more to a westerly direction, passes a cross tracks **(4)** where the path from Erwood comes in from the left. At this crossing point of tracks, anyone starting from Aberedw and wishing to double the length of the walk, could turn left and follow the directions for the Erwood Walk (via points 5, 6 and 7, then back to 4). From the cross tracks, if continuing along the Aberedw Walk, head towards the rocky out-crops. Notice a couple of small pools on the right as we approach the first of the rocky outcrops. Here we bend left and go down quite steeply, then bend right to follow a clear path as its stays close to the rocky outcrops on our right. The highest point of these Aberedw rocks is at 323m (1060ft) Many of the outcrops show thin and hori-zontal bedding with vertical edges, often with vegetation bravely clinging to these slopes in places.

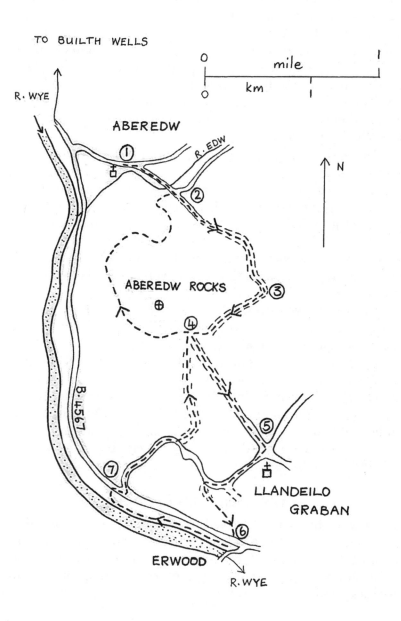

Go on down, to be joined by a path coming in from the left, and we follow the combined path, a grassy track still bending slightly right. When the track begins to bend left, by a Boundary Stone, we fork right as the track divides, to stay close to the rocky outcrops. Views open down to the Wye Valley, with a patch of conifers on the far valley wall. Some larch show up as bare trees in the midst of the dark green in February, but adding lighter touches to the colour later in the year. Just follow the path as its winds through the bracken, steadily descending. Rocky outcrops to our right have piles of scree beneath them, evidence of the ongoing weathering of exposed rocks in the British climate.

A few narrow paths go off our track, but just follow the obvious route ahead, and it will soon bend right to go into the rocks, at the head of a narrow steep valley, almost like a small amphitheatre. We go right alongside the rocks, following the path towards a large gate. We do not go through the gate but keep right with the fence and small field to our left, and a bracken-covered slope up to our right. Pass beneath trees with catkins, and at the end of the field is a small pond, from which a heron flew as we walked past here on our last visit. With a second field on our left, we reach more rocky outcrops, to our right, but we turn left, following the fence. This leads us to some old farm buildings where we join a track, by the farm gate. Turn right here to walk along the track, and when it splits bend sharply left rather than continuing straight ahead, to come on to a stonier track where we turn left, to go through a gate alongside another derelict farm. Follow this track as it winds steadily downhill, and over to the left in the rocks is Llywelyn's Cave. Pass a newly laid hedge (February 2000), go through another gate, and continue along the track as its leads down to another gate, beyond which is the road **(2)**. Turn left here, and retrace steps into Aberedw.

The walk from Erwood

The name of Erwood is derived from 'y rhyd', meaning the ford, which was used by Drovers. This is still an important river crossing, with the ferry and ford of former centuries now replaced by a bridge. The present bridge replaces a 19th-century toll bridge made of iron. There is a picnic area at the old station, where an engine remains as a

The old Erwood station

memorial to the line from Talgarth to Builth. The former waiting room is a very interesting woodturner's studio and craft shop and small café, first opened in 1984.

The walk is 5 miles in length, but can be used to link up with the walk from Aberedw, for a longer walk if required. From near the entrance to the craft shop/café **(6)**, is a gate through which we follow the riverside path (not the Wye Valley Walk), heading upstream, with trees on our left, sloping down to the river. Wild flowers are abundant along here in the spring and the nesting boxes on the trees help to encourage a wide range of birds, including wood warblers and other summer visitors. Down on the river in the winter are a few ducks, as well as dippers, which will be starting to think about nesting at this time of year.

Go through a gate and walk along a narrow path between fences. Descend through trees almost to the river level, cross a small tributary – and if water levels are low enough it will be seen that this is a rocky stretch of river bed, with greenery on islands in mid-stream. Of course, in February it is possible that the river level will be high.

Pass through an area of rhododendrons, over a stile, and straight on, over another stile, as we remain down by the river, with a steep slope up to our right. Reach a few old remnants of buildings and here a path goes left down to the river, at the site of a former ferry. We leave the river side here and go right, up the path through trees, then cross a small field to a gate. Go out on to the road **(7)**, opposite a lone house, and turn right.

Pass the abutments of an old railway bridge, and where a cattle grid crosses the road, we turn left on to a narrow road, and begin to climb. After 100 metres, the road bends sharp right, and we just follow the road, as it climbs up the bracken covered hillside, dotted with a few hawthorn trees. A small stream flows down alongside the road, and on the surrounding hillsides, pipits, yellowhammers and warblers will be singing later in the year. Reach a wood on the right (where bluebells are prolific in the spring) and as the road bends round to the right, look for a stony track turning off to the left. We turn left here and, after about 10 metres, the track splits and we take the right fork, which leads up towards the New House, as it is called! Just before the gate leading to the buildings, turn left, following the track with the fence on our right. The fence ends but we keep straight ahead on to the open hillside, following the green track in a northerly direction. Cross a green track but keep ahead, and soon come alongside a fence on our right, with an improved field of pasture over the fence. The green track continues, between bracken, and the fence turns to the right as we reach the end of the enclosed field, but continue along the path through bracken, as the rocks of Aberedw come into sight.

After 150 metres, a diagonal track crosses our route, and for the return walk we turn sharp right here, and follow the track alongside the opposite boundary of the improved field we walked alongside a few minutes ago. But before taking this return route there is a decision to be made. Walk on for a few more metres to reach a major cross track, which is point (4) on the walk from Aberedw. At this point we can either turn back to complete a walk of 5 miles, or just visit the rocks and then turn back. Alternatively, continue around the route described as the Aberedw Walk, and turn left to walk past and then round the rocks clearly visible to our left. This extension would give us a 10 miler, and we would complete this circuit by coming along the track now to our right.

Whichever choice has been made, from the cross tracks, the journey down to Erwood begins with 50 metres along the path we have just walked, and soon fork left. This leads alongside an improved field, with the fence a few metres to our right. At the end of the field, go through a gate, and straight on along an old green lane between tumbledown walls. Descend steadily and pass to the right of the buildings of Argoed by going through a gate into the farmyard and on to the track. This stony track becomes a narrow surfaced road, and climbs to reach the crossroads in Llandeilo Graban **(5)**. From here, it is possible to walk straight ahead, follow the road as far as the B4594, and then turn right to walk down to Erwood.

Alternatively, and with less walking on roads, we turn right to walk past the church of St Teilo, built of local stone with sandstone window frames. Largely rebuilt in 1897 this church is surrounded by yews and gravestones, and has famous legends about the slaying of Radnorshire's last dragon. There is a path from the south-west corner of the churchyard, where there is a hazardous stone step stile. This path leads alongside three fields to join a track passing Nelfa

St Teilo church in Llandeilo Graban

and winding down to Erwood, but we selected to walk along the road. After a quarter mile where the road has a sharp right bend, notice through a gate on the left the remnants of the old track used by horse and cart traffic in former years, and leading to Nelfa. Continue down the road for a further 200 metres, to another right bend, and here turn left through the gate, and follow the grassy path going left through the bracken and down the hill. The path leads fairly steeply down to reach the road very close to the Erwood Station Craft Centre and car park **(6)**.

March

Hereford, Breinton, The Weir Gardens and the Kempley area

Four walks of varying length, include three located near Hereford, and the fourth at Kempley in Gloucestershire. They pass through glorious countryside, walking round lanes, fields and woods as well as along the banks of the Wye.

Lengths of walks: the options are a 5-mile (2 hours) walk round the fields and country lanes from Breinton, or a 6-mile (2-3 hours) walk along the river bank from Hereford to Breinton (and back). These two can be joined together if required, starting from either of the two points. A separate walk is the tour of the wonderful gardens of The Weir GR435418 (charge for admission unless a member of the National Trust), for which 1-2 hours will be required. The length of the daffodil walk is 8 miles, with a short cut option of 5½ miles.

Terrain: for all of these walks the terrain is gently undulating, but likely to be muddy in March.

Maps: the Hereford and Breinton walks can be found on Landranger map 149 and on Explorer 189. The Daffodil walk around the Kempley and Dymock area is on Landranger 149 and on Explorer 189, extending on to Outdoor Leisure 14.

Starting point: Hereford, where there are several car parks (payment necessary) or at Breinton church GR473395. The starting point for the daffodil walk is GR677284, this point is reached via Much Marcle, from the A449, or via Dymock.

Public transport: limited except for Hereford which is easily accessible by bus or train, and Dymock has a regular bus service.

Facilities: information is available from the Tourist Information Centres in Hereford (phone 01432 268430) or in Newent (phone 01531 822468). A wide choice of refreshments is available in Hereford, and there are pubs along the main A438 near Sugwas and Swainshill. Teas are served in Kempley village hall at weekends during the daffodil season.

Weather

Named after Mars, the Roman god of war, the variable nature of this month should encourage walkers to be ready for any kind of weather. All four seasons can be experienced in one day, and wind direction is a good guide as to the type of weather arriving in Britain. The old saying of: *March comes in like a lion, and goes out like a lamb* can sometimes be true, and this year (1999) began wet and windy, but mild, until a brief northerly spell began on the 4th. A high pressure system out to the west gave a strong wind with snow showers in the north, and occasional snow flurries even in the Wye Valley where the daily maxima were 6-7°C. The ground was still very damp and cold, with some flooding occurring. Temperatures remained cool for several days, with sharp frost during the second week of the month. The weather turned milder and sunny on the 14th and a spring-like spell for several days brought on more bird song and plant growth. Temperatures reached 17-19°C in many places and remained quite warm, until the end of the month, with the exception of a couple of cold northerly days around the 19th and 26th. A very mild end to the month, led up to the Easter weekend, by which time it was generally considered that spring was two weeks earlier than average.

The Countryside

A milder than average month ensured that the signs of spring were well under way early in the month. Rooks were at their nests (e.g. at the rookery in The Weir) and many of the garden and hedgerow birds were seen chasing each other as the prelude to pairing off and mating. Blackbirds were nest-building and rooks were carrying sticks, either gathered honestly or stolen from neighbours. The Mistle thrush is already well into its breeding season, as seen at The

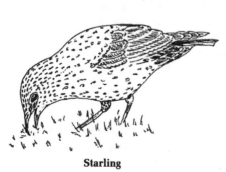

Starling

Weir. Bird song steadily increased as any mild day encouraged the birds to pretend it was spring. Green woodpeckers are to be heard calling and the great spotted woodpecker may be heard drumming. A noisy singer is the starling, my **bird of the month**, and in the midst of its assortment of screeches

and whistles are some pleasant notes as well as remarkable imper-
sonations of other noises. The male sings to attract a mate, and may
even start to build a rough nest. His appearance, like the song, is
often underrated, as the dull blackness is a mixture of very bright
greens, blue and purple when seen at close quarters. Breeding birds
get a yellow beak, with the male having a blue base to the bill and the
female a pink base. Legs become brighter too. Whereas some starlings are paired, others are still in flocks and probably have not yet
got their yellow bills. These will be the European migrants, here for
the winter, and not yet ready to return to their breeding areas in cli-
mates colder than England. Huge flocks are to be seen in the winter,
although numbers are thought to have declined in recent years. Just
before these starlings leave for their summer haunts, our summer
visitors will be arriving, and a few chiffchaffs are likely to have been
heard by the end of the month.

Hawthorn hedges show green in increasing amounts as the days
tick by, and a few trees are also showing first signs of green, notably
the horse chestnut with its sticky buds. Lots of pussy willows grow
near the River Wye, and bankside weeping willows are showing
their first signs of greenery. A few trees are brightened by blossom,
and A.C. Swinburne wrote:

> And in green underwood and cover,
> Blossom by blossom the spring began.

In the Wye valley several recently ploughed fields are reddish
brown, vaguely reminiscent of Devon with its more famous reddish
soils. The similarity is related to the similarity of the geology, the
rocks in both areas being of Devonian or Old Red Sandstone age. A
few winter crops are already growing, but many of the fields are still
very wet. More of the fields are green however, as this is predomi-
nantly a grazing area, and sheep and lambs are numerous.

Wild flowers are making this a yellow month, both on the field
margins and in the gardens. Daffodils are prolific, and one may
wonder how many million there are in England and Wales. Lesser
celandines too may be numerous as they seem to appear very suddenly in large numbers in the middle of the month. Primroses too,
their name derived from 'prima rosa', the first rose, with variety of
colour provided by the blue and white of violets. With the appear-

ance of the first flowers, there are soon the first bees, of the large bumble variety, looking for nesting sites, and an occasional peacock butterfly makes an appearance on the sunnier days. Frogs and toads spawn in many locations.

The Weir Gardens

The Weir estate was owned by Mr. Roger Parr, a Manchester Banker, and about 174 ha. (430 acres) were given to the National Trust in 1959. The magnificent 18th-century house is not open to the public, but the gardens are open from mid-February until the end of October, daily, but excluding Mondays and Tuesdays. They are situated on a steep, south-facing valley side, overlooking the Wye and the garden was laid out by Mr. Parr, mainly in the 1920s. He also embanked the river and laid out the paths. In this very sheltered valley the spring flowers are early and clothe much of the floor, beneath a variety of trees and shrubs. At the far end of the garden is small wood, containing a rookery, likely to be noisy during March. In addition to the flowers and shrubs, there is a wealth of bird life, with tree creepers, nuthatches, woodpeckers and tits, with warblers and redstarts in the summer. On the river are ducks, as well as kingfishers, and in the summer, sand martins.

Dymock Daffodils

The area around Dymock and Kempley is still famous for its wild daffodils although there are fewer than in the past. The Daffodil Way is a 10-mile circular path opened in 1988 by Windcross Public Paths Project and we are following a section of this route though also using several other paths which criss cross this area. Our walk can also take in the remarkable churches at Kempley. A special Daffodil Weekend is organised, generally near the end of March.

In former times many pickers came to the area to gather up the daffodils for sale in the towns, and John Masefield wrote:

> *And there the pickers come, picking for town*
> *Those dancing daffodils; all day they pick;*
> *Hard featured women, weather-beaten brown,*
> *Or swarthy-red, the colour of old brick.*

The daffodils are now all protected and it is illegal to pick them. The Dymock Poets (see January, page 12) observed and wrote about the wild daffodils, and it was Lascelles Abercrombie who wrote:

> *From Marcle way,*
> *From Dymock, Kempley, Newent, Bromsberrow,*
> *Redmarley, all the meadowland daffodils seem*
> *Running in golden tides to Ryton Firs.*

Kempley

The Norman church of St Mary's was built of local sandstone in the early 12th century, and was the parish church for Kempley. As the village gradually moved away towards higher ground, the new church of St Edward was built in 1903. The west door of St Mary's

Lych gate of St Edward's church

Sculpted relief at St Edward's

dates from the 12th century and was the outside door, until the tower (built for defensive purposes) was added about 1276. The Tree of Life tympanum over the south door is almost hidden by the porch – but is very similar to the one found in Dymock church. The frescoes in St Mary's date from 1130-1140 and are reckoned to be some of the oldest and finest in Britain .They were covered at the time of the Reformation and remained hidden until 1872, and were restored in 1955. The church was given to the nation in 1977 and is managed by the Department of the Environment. The timber roof of St Mary has been accurately dated by dendrochronologists and is known to be the oldest roof (religious or secular) in Britain, and one of the oldest in Europe.

Hereford

This small city, no more than a market town really, has been a settlement since pre-Roman times, and was the capital of Saxon Mercia. Located at an ancient ford across the river, a bridge was later built at the same site. King Offa chose a location near the crossing point for a chapel, and the Cathedral, begun in 1079 is on the same site. This magnificent building is perhaps most noted for its 13th-century world map, the Mappa Mundi and its large medieval chained library. Almost

River Wye and Hereford cathedral

as important and as historic as the Cathedral is the Church of All Saints, with its twisted spire. This church dates mostly from the 13th and 14th centuries and also has a chained library, though smaller than that in the cathedral. The old bridge across the Wye is from the 15th century, the same age as some remnants of the city wall, and the Old House, a timber framed building in the town centre dates from 1621. Famous names associated with the city include Nell Gwynne, who is remembered by a plaque in Gwynne Street, and Bulmers, the famous cider producer.

Breinton Walk

Start from Breinton N.T. car park **(1)** near the Breinton spring, and the church of St Michael, a stone building with a small slate tower. The church is in a delightful rural setting, and there has been a church on the site since the 12th century. A Norman window can still be seen in the nave, but the present building mostly dates from 1860s – rebuilt by F.R. Kempson. Two large yew trees in the churchyard are very ancient. A small mound near the church is the remnant of the earthworks of a medieval moated house. Just below the car park down by the river bank is the spring which flows continuously from the sandstone outcrop – and is fresh and safe to drink.

From the car park, walk back along the lane and just beyond the driveway to Breinton House, with its gate posts topped by iron stags' heads. Go left through an iron kissing gate and diagonally across two small fields where we shall probably see the first blossom on the walk – but more will be seen

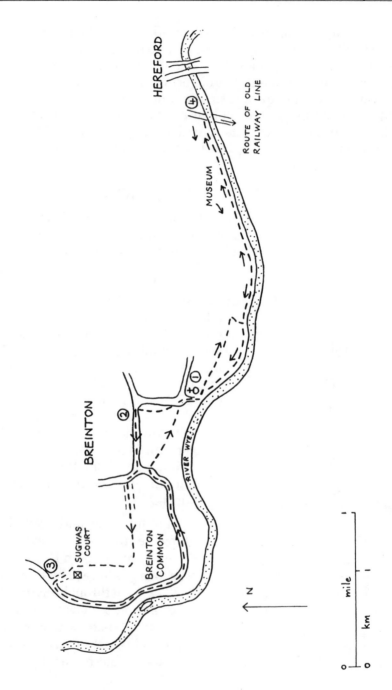

later. Then go on through the gate and straight ahead along the driveway, passing the gate into Breinton Court on the left. At the end of the short grassy track, go left through an iron gate. The Wye Valley Walk (our return route) stays along the left side of the field, but we follow the hedge on the right margin of the field, soon to reach a stile and the narrow country road, where we turn left **(2)**.

The road descends slightly into Upper Breinton, and at the fork turn right towards Swainshill and Stretton Sugwas, to pass a couple of old houses on the right with flowering aubretia, before reaching a track and bridleway going left. This is our route, on the Wye Valley Walk, passing to the left of the Manor House as we follow the track between fields. Celandines and daffodils are likely to be giving some yellow colour to this track.

Reach a large metal gate, and keep straight ahead into the open field and up and over the top of this small hill, enjoying the good views, especially to the left. Walk to a gate at the far side of the field (with the 114 metres triangulation point a few metres to our right), and keep ahead, with a hedge on our left. As we descend slightly, notice the white house away in the distance to the north-west, sitting at the top of a small river cliff. This is The Weir, with the wooded Garnons Hill beyond, on which a short remnant of Offa's Dyke has survived. Further to the right is Credenhill Park Wood, another wooded hill, but this one has an old fort on its summit.

Descend slightly to a stile in the corner of the field, go over this and immediately right over a second stile, and turn right to follow a path through the woods. A carpet of bluebells will be growing on the wooded slope down to the left, and there may be a few in flower by the end of the month. Leave the wood over a stile and take the left of the two paths, diagonally across the field, admiring the views to the Wye Valley on the left, as we go. Reach another stile and head across this large field to another stile and then on down to the far left corner of this next field. There is a small pond with a dam on our right, and we reach a stile on the left margin of the field, which is the route of our path through the woods. The small stream is on our right, and this wood is floored with snowdrops, which may be past their best by the end of the month. Reach a stile and go into a field, with Sugwas Court to the left. Built of brick in about 1800, this is situated on the foundations of a house belonging to the Bishops of Hereford, and remnants of an old Norman arch can be seen in the stable block.

Cross the field containing some magnificent old trees, a few clumps of daffodils and a yellow splash of winter aconites. Reach a stile and go over to the drive, turning right to walk out to the road by the Lodge (3). Turn left along this quiet country lane, walking between orchards at first and then open fields. The orchards are frequented by as many as five members of the thrush family – blackbird, redwings, fieldfare, song thrush and mistle thrush. Here, as elsewhere on this walk, mistletoe is quite common in many of the trees.

Continue along the lane with its wide verges, passing between fields of grass, with an occasional cropped field, to reach an isolated dwelling, formerly a pub, the Boat Inn. The river is just a few metres away to the right, and across on the other bank is a modern large brick house, and an old thatched house on stilts to overcome flood problems. The road climbs gradually, to come up into the small village of Breinton Common. (On the left is Wadworth Cottage, with a memorial to Alice Wadworth under the overhang – January 1st 1901) Pass between the houses, with many attractive gardens, already becoming colourful, so early in the year. An old iron milepost, saying Hereford 4 and Sugwas 0, is a relic of the former toll road from Hereford to Sugwas Passage, where a ferry used to cross the river to Lower Eaton, near the Boat Inn. Next we pass Chapel House on the right, with its lovely views down to the river, and the red cliff on the opposite side of the river, after which the house called Red Rocks has been named. Beyond the left bend in the road, we reach the magnificent modernised old barn and granary. Then, after two sharp bends, look for our path going off to the right, over a ditch and up a few steps to a stile. Once over the stile turn right, staying close to the field margin, to a stile at the far edge of the field, and then along the right margin of the next field, with good views to Breinton Court on the right. Go through the iron gate and turn right along the grassy lane to pass Breinton Court Lodge on the left, with its colourful garden, and retrace steps across the two small fields to the narrow road. Straight across here is a stile and footpath, which may be used for the walk to Hereford, but we turn right if we wish to return to the N.T. car park near the church and Breinton Spring (1).

Hereford to Breinton walk

This is 6 miles of very gentle walking, taking from 2-3 hours. Starting from Hereford we find the large road bridge over the Wye (4), with the old stone bridge a few metres downstream, and descend to the surfaced path on the south side of the river. After about 500 metres, cross the river on the old Great Western railway bridge and continue upstream on the north side of the river. The path is surfaced for a short distance, as we pass the playing fields of Hereford Cathedral School on the right. Pass (or visit) the interesting Waterworks Museum, and the miniature railway line and just keep heading westwards along the riverside path. The golf course will be noticed across on the other bank, and we just plod on, over a couple of newish gated footbridges. When we reach a wooden kissing gate there is just one more field to cross to reach Breinton. At the end of this field are a large gate and a small kissing gate, and the path up to the car park and church is a broad track. Before going up here, just go a few more metres alongside the river to look at the amazing spring, flowing with cool fresh water from the sandstone rocks on the valley side. Go up to the car park (1) and the narrow road, with church over to the right. This car park is an alternative starting point.

From the car park, continue along the narrow lane to the gateway with stags' heads on the gateposts to Breinton House and the kissing gate on the route of the Breinton Walk on the left. On the right is a tall stile over which we go, following the Wye Valley Walk signs, and head diagonally right across the orchard to another stile. Then turn left towards the church, with bright yellow of lesser celandine and daffodils in the churchyard. Pass to the right of the churchyard to reach an iron kissing gate in the corner of the field. Look out for the white violets near this gate, and along the path as we proceed flowers are numerous, with many white and purple violets.

A wood on the steep slopes to the right is floored with wild flowers – bluebells coming out before the end of the month – and on the left is the large lawn and clear views to the Old Vicarage. Next on the left is an orchard, with clumps of mistletoe and the first signs of leaves just peeping out before the end of the month. There may be sheep and lambs in the old tradition of grazing sheep in orchards.

The path reaches a stile and we proceed along the right margin of a field, by the hedge, looking for a stile which takes us out of the field and we turn left to follow the hedge on the other side. Once we reach Warham House on the left, turn right to descend the slope along a worn track, and walk alongside the tiny stream towards the river. Note the golf course and Belmont Hotel on the other side of the river. Reach the small stile on to the riverside path and turn left. Cross over the small stream, using a new gated footbridge, and follow the river. The path leads us between the river and grassy fields, and on or near the river we may see ducks, chiffchaff, tits, finches, a tree creeper or even a kingfisher – and many other birds in the summer. The trees too are interesting, with willows just sprouting, and alder with small catkins and small cones. Evidence of recent flooding is likely, with straw or branches deposited in riverside trees or in the fields.

Pass another gated bridge, and views to the water tower and cathedral will open up, as we walk between the river and cropped fields for the next half mile. We reach the miniature railway and Broomy Hill Junction and the Water Works Museum on our left, but keep straight ahead. Houses increase on both side of the river as we approach Hereford, and at the old railway bridge we continue along the north side the river until the path ends. Turn left and then right to follow roads up to the main road, beyond which is our route back to the centre of the city. Down to the right is the modern road bridge over the River Wye.

Kempley Walk

Start at the Forestry Commission car park (1) in Queen's Wood GR 677284. Walk back on to the road and turn left, to walk out of the woods and reach the first houses on the edge of Kempley Green. Lots of daffodils will be seen and bird song is to be heard all around. Just past the first house on the right, turn right along a driveway and after about 10 metres, go right along the path between hedges, and over a stile into a field. Follow the hedge along the field margin, and notice the views to Malvern Hills away to the left. Descend to a small hollow, go over a stile, and keep straight ahead. Ignore the path going off to the left, by a large barn, and keep straight ahead to go on through a gate. Follow the slight holloway downhill to a small stream and large willow tree, as we cross the field to aim for a stile leading into Dymock Wood.

Follow the path through the woods, rich in wild daffodils, and bird life including pheasants. Reach a gravel track but keep straight ahead, still following the footpath sign of a yellow arrow with black spot, indicating we are on the Daffodil Way. The clear track winds through the woods, and can often be muddy at this time of year. Reach a broad track where we turn left, passing a few conifers on the right, and noisy drone of traffic on the M50. Pass a few flowering

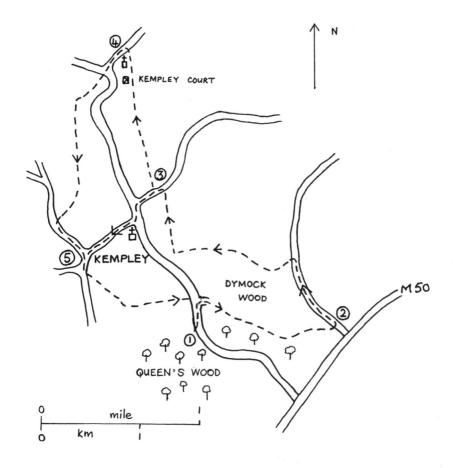

gorse bushes, and several trees laden with catkins, as we descend slightly to a narrow road, where we turn left **(2)**.

Follow this road through the woods, and out to open fields, to reach a large house on our right, with a pond in the garden, a small orchard and blossoming prunus trees, then look for a footpath to the left. Go over the stile and cross the field to another stile in the wooden fence, and pass to the right of a small pond, walking on the causeway which creates this pond. The bushes in and around the pond include some bright red dogwood shrubs.

Go on through a gate and after about 20 metres turn right to cross the stiled footbridge and into a field. We have seen daffodils in woods, roadsides, the middle of fields and here they are abundant around the edges of the fields. Cross the field to a stile and then go right alongside the hedge. At the end of this field go over the fence or gate, turn right for a few metres and then left through a small gate, to pass to the right of the duck pond. Walk up the right margin of this field, with a small valley to our left and much evidence of rabbits. Reach a stile in the corner, then go straight ahead across the middle of the next field, to a stile and another field. After this, a stile and footbridge leads us into the next small field and then another stile as we follow the field margin on our left. At the end of this field a footpath sign points straight ahead through the gate, but we turn right, to follow the hedge. Near the end of this field go left into the next field but still continue alongside the hedge, now on our right. Go over a stile, and follow the field margin, to reach a stile by a large gate, and the narrow road, where we turn left.

About 100 metres along this road, there is a stile on the right **(3)** and the **Main Walk** turns here.

Short Cut

For a walk of 5½ miles, as opposed to 8 miles, keep straight ahead along the road. Turn left at the T-junction and walk between the houses of Kempley to reach the church, where we turn right.

St Edward's church dates from 1903 and is linked with the Arts and Crafts movement. It was built of local materials, sandstone and wood from the Forest of Dean, by local craftsmen, as suggested by Lord Beauchamp. Randall Wells was in charge of the work, and it was he who designed the three sculpted stone reliefs. There is a small tower, and an impressive stone lych gate, with its two small gates separated by a stone pillar. Daffodils grow all over the church-yard

Walk on down the road, passing the church on our left, and at the T-junction in Fishpool, turn left **(5)**. The **Main Walk** comes in from the right here to join the route of this short cut. After about 100 metres, go left over a stile and follow the right margin of the field to another stile. Go on over this and keep straight ahead following the hedge and fence on the right, for several fields, then go straight across the middle of another field and heading to the right of the large house clearly visible ahead. Cross a footbridge with a gate, to pass to the right of the stables, and then cross the driveway to the left, following the Daffodil Way sign to a sensible stile. Walk along the right margin of the field, with the large Moor House on our right, to a footbridge over the ditch and on into the next field. Cross the middle of the next field, to reach a stiled footbridge, and continue straight ahead alongside the hedge on our left to a double stile. Keep straight ahead, climbing gently up to a gate and the road in Kempley Green.

Turn right along the road that will lead us back to our starting point in Queen's Wood.

Main Walk

The right turn takes us over a stile and along the right side of a large field, following the line of a small stream and a hedge to our right. At the end of a large field there is a stile, and a gate, and we keep ahead, along the right margin of the next field. We can see, over to our left, very clear views of the black and white front of Kempley Court, a painted brick farm house with a date of 1689 and a crest on the wall. We pass to the right of all the buildings, through a large gate, a farm-yard and then another large gate, to head across the next field straight towards St Mary's church. Our path leads to a stiled foot-bridge over Kempley Brook, the cause of flooding in the past, and then across a small field to a gate and into the churchyard **(4)**, with its colourful daffodils, and many tombs including a few table tombs. This church is magnificent and one of the most interesting small churches in England and Wales.

Leave St Mary's churchyard and turn left along the narrow road, with the church and then Kempley Court to our left. At the T-junction there is a small island with a memorial tree and a plaque which reads 'This tree was planted on the 20th day of February in 1893 by the Vicar and Parishioners of Kempley in commemoration of the coming of age of William 7th Earl of Beauchamp, Madresfield Court, Worcestershire.'

Go straight across the road here, over the stile and across the middle of the field, passing close to the left-hand of the two telegraph poles. Follow the line of wires from this pole to reach the far side of the field, then turn right for a few metres and turn left through a gate and across the ditch. Ignore the footbridge to the left, but walk straight ahead along the field margin, with Kempley Brook to our left. Pass a farm bridge going over the stream but continue along the field margin to a stile at the end of the field.

Turn left here, following the stream on our left, and reach a stile and footbridge over a tributary, and still keep ahead. Pass another farm bridge on our left, across which is a stile and a stone memorial to A.W. Money Kyrle, October 28, 1908. We continue to follow the stream, go over a stile and straight on, noting the clumps of ramsons alongside the stream, just before we reach a stile and the road.

Turn left along the road to walk past the Kempley sign and the large buildings of Hill Brook Farm perched up to our left. Soon, you reach the road junction **(5)**, where the Short Cut route comes in from the left, from Kempley Green and Dymock. We turn right towards Upton Bishop, Linton and Ross, and follow the directions given in the Short Cut section above.

April

Tintern

The glorious riverside, old broadleaved woods and steep valley sides combine to make up these invigorating walks, with the added bonus of a visit to Tintern Abbey.

Lengths of walks: Brockweir and Devil's Pulpit is about 7 miles, requiring 3-4 hours, with longer if stopping at the Old Railway Station or elsewhere en route. On the other side of the valley, there is a shorter walk to Penterry church and the Glyn Woods of nearly 5 miles, requiring 2-3 hours. The two walks could be combined with a mid-point break for refreshment in Tintern.

Terrain: each walk includes a very steep climb out of the valley, and also the return descent. There are certain to be muddy patches in the woods and near the river.

Map: O.S. Outdoor Leisure 14, Wye Valley and Forest of Dean, or Landranger 162.

Starting point: the Abbey GR533001, where there is a large parking space.

Public Transport: bus service runs along the valley from Chepstow and Monmouth (Mondays to Saturdays).

Facilities: nearest towns are Chepstow (Tourist Information Centre phone number 01291 623772) and Monmouth (Tourist Information Centre phone number 01600 713899). Good choice of pubs and restaurants in Tintern.

Weather

Winter weather systems are often still experienced in April but with the beginnings of the summer systems showing signs of developing. The jet streams are less active than in the winter, and can meander further north or south than their average location. This is likely to cause the rapid fluctuations for which the month is noted.

Spring takes two steps forward and one backward is true in most years. April in 1999 had more warm spells than cold spells and the rainy periods were longer than the dry periods. It was a warmer than average month (the warmest for ten years in many places), with temperatures up to 20°C during the final few days. The month began with nearly two weeks of south-westerly or south-easterly air, with another wet and changeable spell near the end of the month. This contributed to a wetter than average month, especially in the west of England and in Wales. Predictions have been made that no hose pipe bans will be necessary this summer after a series of wetter than average months. A cold spell occurred in mid-month, bringing night frosts and also a day of heavy snowfall, coinciding with the start of the cricket season. There was no real spell of easterly weather, which is quite unusual, and contributed to the warmer than average month. Vegetation growth was considered about two weeks ahead of average – although perhaps the average is now changing!

The Countryside

By mid-month, valley sides near the Wye were a mixture of colours, with some light green as new leaves were emerging on deciduous broadleaved trees and, on the larch, a few patches of white blossom. Many trees still bare – though by the end of the month these are mostly covered in growth. One exception is the ash, still showing last year's keys, but no leaves.

Fields on the valley floor are mostly in grass, with flocks of sheep and young lambs as well as a few groups of cattle on the lush green pastures. Debris, still visible along the banks, provides evidence of the recent flooding and many sandbags were lying around on the roadsides and near buildings. Just one or two fields contain young crops, including an occasional splash of yellow of a rape field, and one or two ploughed fields are still bare. As the river is tidal up as far as Brockweir, muddy banks showing if tide is low, will have a thin coating of chocolate-coloured mud.

Bird life to be seen on the river include swans, ducks, gulls and possibly a cormorant. Pied wagtails and jackdaws are active in the Abbey ruins. Pied wagtails (my **bird of the month)** are widespread and very versatile, living in hilly areas, pastoral farm-

Pied wagtail

land, towns or by riversides, and ceaselessly bob their tails – nodtails rather than wagtails. Males and females are quite similar though the females have a greyer back than the male and a slightly smaller bib. Black and white colouring, twittering call and undulating flight make them readily recognisable. In recent years, many groups of pied wagtails have been flying into towns to communal roosts during the winter months. Many of the wagtails are resident, and by April most varieties of resident birds are singing lustily, and this bird song increases as plant growth quickens. Early summer migrants are appearing, especially later in the month and the first house martins of the year may be seen flying along the river. Chiffchaffs are certain to be heard signalling their arrival with their welcome but somewhat repetitive song. Many summer visitors did arrive in the first two weeks, when the weather was mild, but were caught out by the sharp frosts of mid-month – as were some of the resident birds that had nested rather early.

In the milder spells early and later in the month, small swarms of insects are out and about – gnats or midges in the sunny periods, but few caterpillars or other food for chicks hatched too soon.

Flower life increases rapidly, and there is a yellow start to the month, with daffodils, celandines, dandelions and primroses, plus a few violets to give variety of colour. By mid-month, white ramson flowers line the roadsides as well as ladies smock and some cowslips. Bluebells cover the floor of several patches of woodland, and often occur with stitchwort. Cow parsley on the roadsides gives a whiteness to the roadsides, and by the end of the month the green candles on the horse chestnut were showing their white. Hawthorn and blackthorn add to the whiteness in many hedges. April's name is derived from *aperire*, meaning to open, and this applies to much of the plant life, as *'spring is bursting out all over.'*

Tintern

Wordsworth is reputed to have been an ardent admirer of the Wye valley, and whilst staying at Llandogo in 1798, he wrote his "Lines composed a few miles above Tintern Abbey", which included the quote *Oh sylvan Wye, thou wanderer thro' the woods.*

The village consists of the two older settlements of Tintern Parva in the north and Chapel Hill in the south, and is mainly a thin ribbon along the west side of the river. The Cistercians arrived in 1131 and they farmed in the surrounding countryside – mainly for sheep – on large estates stretching down the valley, up the hills to the west and across to the Severn in the east. It is rumoured that the Monks, and the Romans before them, had grown vines here, and there is certainly a modern vineyard in the north of the village. The Monks developed industries that continued in the village, which had become a minor industrial centre by the 17th century, with wire works, furnaces and forges. The wire working had begun in the 16th century, using some German expertise, and making good use of local water power. A plaque commemorates that this was the first place in Britain to make brass, in 1568. The last remnant of mills is to be seen at the Abbey Mill. Local water power came from Fedw Brook, which flows into the River Angedy. This became an important iron-producing area – until the 19th century when most of the forges closed – because of the development of steam power elsewhere, especially in the South Wales coalfield region. Then tourism was the next economic development, aided by the motor car. The parish church of St Michael is at the northern end of the village, on the site of a Celtic church built in 765. There has been a church on the site ever since, and the present church includes a few medieval fragments, including the font, but it was enlarged and improved in 1846, and is really a Victorian church.

The Old Station

The railway line was opened in 1876 and closed in 1964. The old railway station is one mile north of the village and has been converted into a visitor centre (open from Easter to October) with a small café, gift shop and exhibitions. Several special events are organised here during the summer and it makes an excellent starting point for walks along the river valley. There are parking (pay and display) and picnic areas, but no real trains, just old carriages, a signal box and signals. A small model train often runs here during the summer.

Tintern – the abbey and village

Tintern Abbey

One of Britain's finest monastic ruins, in a wonderful setting, the Abbey was the subject of a famous painting by Turner in 1795. Cistercian Monks, who wore white, moved here in 1131, when the abbey was founded by Walter Fitz Richard of Clare, Lord of Lower Gwent. In 1270, Roger Bigod, the Earl of Norfolk rebuilt much of the abbey, and the remains of that abbey can still be seen today. The walls are nearly intact, but no roof survived. The abbey had become quite poor and was dissolved in 1536, by Henry VIII. The abbey is open daily, and excellent information boards outline the history. The abbey was built of Carboniferous and Devonian rocks, mainly Tintern sandstone. The Monks quarried stone, but also dug for iron ore, hence the furnace nearby.

The longer walk: Brockweir and Devil's Pulpit

From the Abbey car park **(1)**, walk along the river bank going upstream, passing the modern bungalows built on the former site of the quay. From here, we move away from the river passing a small chapel, and reaching the main road opposite the Royal George Hotel. Turn right along here past the Abbey Mill and follow the road through the main part of the village, almost as far as the church. As the road bends left, a sign pointing to the right will lead us past St Michael's Church and on to the Wye Valley Walk towards Brockweir Bridge.

Leave the churchyard through a wooden gate, and walk along the field margin, with the river just to our right. This part of the walk is often flooded during the winter, but a detour along the road is possible. Reach the point where the old railway line crossed the river, and climb up the steps on to the former line passing through a small woodland area, rich in wild flowers, wood anemones, primroses and violets. Turn left along the railway line, to walk into the old Station, now an interesting tourist point and well worth looking round. Refreshments are available here if required.

Continue beyond the station, either going right through a gate to walk alongside the river, or, if damp, just follow the line of the railway. Both paths lead to the same point where we climb steps up to the road, and turn right to walk across the bridge into Brockweir **(2)**.

The old Station

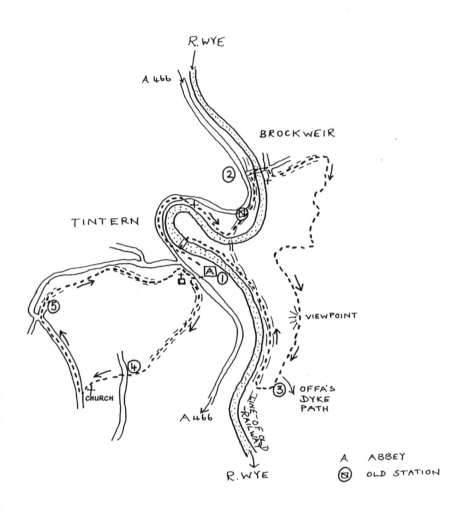

R. WYE

A 466

BROCKWEIR

②

TINTERN

+

Ⓢ

A

①

VIEWPOINT

⑤

④

CHURCH

③ OFFA'S
DYKE
PATH

A 466

LINE OF OLD RAILWAY

R. WYE

A   ABBEY

Ⓢ   OLD STATION

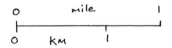

0   mile   1

0   KM   1

↑N

This bridge dates from 1904, and until that time there was a ferry at this point. Note Brockweir's slipway into the river, on the left side of the bridge. It was near here, at the upper limit of tides, that shipbuilding and repairing took place. Cargoes were unloaded from sea-going boats on to the river trows to continue their journey upstream, as far as Hereford. Pubs were numerous in those days, but only one now remains in Brockweir.

Pass the Brockweir Country Inn on the right, and turn right along the narrow road. After a few metres, a narrow path leads to the Moravian Church and although our route is really going straight ahead, it is worth a short detour to this church, founded in 1831 by Moravian Missionaries based in Bristol. In the churchyard is the grave of Flora Klickman, who edited 'The Girls Own Paper' and 'Woman's Magazine', as well as writing about the beauties of the Wye Valley in which she lived. She died in 1958, aged 92.

Retrace steps back to the narrow road, which will lead us through a farmyard, passing a few stables on the left, and then turning left, following the sign for the Offa's Dyke Path. This leads past more stables along a track, which climbs steadily. Reach a large gate beyond which we are in an open field, with a hedge on our right and a sloping field dropping to the small stream down to our left. Just before reaching a ruined stone barn is a three prong signpost all pointing for the Offa's Dyke path. We go slightly right, signed to Madgett Hill – ¼, along a stony track between small trees, many of which are showing their roots.

Go over a stile by a gate and turn right, then after about 30 metres go diagonally left to head up the slope towards the trees – accompanied by the noise of sheep, lambs and perhaps buzzards – with fine views all around. A post at the top of the grass points us to the left for about 20 metres and then sharp right to climb up through trees and rocks to reach the top of the hill, where we turn right. We are now walking along the line of Offa's Dyke. Walk along an embankment, with open fields to the right, and although fairly level, Offa's Dyke path for the next mile or so has numerous short ups and downs as well as meanders.

Reach a stile and notice about the Tidenham section of Offa's Dyke, managed by English Heritage for the next two miles. (The notice makes comments about King Offa – King of Mercia 757-790 – who built this dyke to establish a frontier between his kingdom and the Welsh – see Introduction, page 2).

The path goes near the edge of the woods, and has a flooring of ramsons here and elsewhere along the walk. There are numerous other wild flowers too, notably lesser celandine, wood anemones, as well as violets and bluebells. Reach a cross paths and keep straight ahead through the asymmetric barrier to keep out horses and/or motor bikes. The trees are mainly deciduous and views open up to the right, though these are very restricted once all the leaves have grown on the trees. Early April is a wonderful time to follow this walk. After a stretch in the woods, the path leads out to the edge again, with a grassy field to the left, as we walk round the top of a steep valley. Then once again the pathway drifts into the woods and the white Brockweir bridge is visible a long way down to the right.

Reach a signpost pointing right to Tintern 1 mile, but we go straight ahead towards 'Devil's Pulpit ½' – and on we go. The path leads to the edge of the woods again, where a stile and path go left, but we continue along Offa's Dyke path. Devil's Pulpit is another 100 metres, and from this lump of limestone the views down to the Abbey ruins are magnificent. Legend has it that the Devil preached from here to try to lure the monks into bad habits, and sell their souls to him – but with little success.

Continue along the Offa's Dyke to reach the Memorial seat to Chris Pugh (Wye Valley Warden 1972-1983), where more views through the trees look down to the valley. Continue along the path, which is very stony in this section, and as we descend a little, an open field is visible to the left. Shortly after passing the end of this field, the main path turns left, and we leave Offa's Dyke here to go slightly right **(3)**, following a footpath arrow, and descend steeply through trees. The path leads down to a few steps and at the bottom of this slope reaches a fairly horizontal path, where we turn left, and begin to climb slightly. After about 100 metres, turn right off this path, still following yellow arrows, to descend through holly and brambles. The path opens out as we keep going, steadily downhill, to reach a forestry track. We go straight across the track, following the yellow arrow, and along another track, still descending, to pass a few redwoods on the right. Many more conifers are growing in this part of the woods. As the track levels off slightly, we leave it by turning right very sharply (an elbow turning), still following a yellow arrow and descend to another track, where we turn right.

This is the route of the old railway, and is naturally very gentle walking, for the 2 miles back to our starting point. We walk through delightful woodlands, with wild flowers, butterflies and birds in abundance. Peacock and brimstone butterflies were dancing all around the last time I walked through here on a sunny day early in April, and the brimstones on the ground looked almost like the primroses which were in flower at the time. After a mile or so, the river comes into sight, down to our left, and then we reach the opening into the tunnel, where the railway cut through the valley side. Here we fork slightly left to follow the route of the old link line leading into Tintern to the Wire Factory.

Just beyond this is an alternative path leading down to the river, but we continue along the line of the railway, and soon reach the point where a cobbled path goes up to the right, signposted to Brockweir and Devil's Pulpit; to the left there is another path down to the river bank. But, keeping straight ahead, we soon reach the railway bridge where we cross the river. This old bridge was built in 1872 to connect the Tintern Wire Works with the new railway from Chepstow to Monmouth. Walk back into Tintern, turn left along the road, pass the mill, and then fork left off the road to pass the old chapel. Retrace your steps to the starting point by the Abbey.

The shorter walk

This is from Tintern Abbey to Penterry church, through Glyn woods and the ruins of St Mary's.

Cross the road from the entrance to the Abbey (1) and follow the Wye Valley Walk sign along the narrow road going to the right. After a few metres, at the T-junction, we turn left along a stony track to walk behind houses and the Beaufort Hotel. Once past the buildings the track splits, left to Reddings Farm, or straight on into the woods. This is the Wye Valley Walk signposted to Penterry Lane, and we follow this stony track as it climbs steadily for half a mile up through the woods. The woods are floored by an abundance of wild flowers, notably ramsons (allium ursinum – allium is the Latin for garlic) but also lesser celandine, violets and bluebells. There is also a wealth of bird life. A stream flows just to the left of the path, and it is amazing to think that this small stream is responsible for cutting the deep valley in which we are walking. The stream suddenly shrinks in volume as we pass a spring, and we climb up to an exposed outcrop, where the track is on solid rock for a few metres, not just the loose rocks seen lower down. About 60 metres beyond this rocky area, the Wye Valley Walk turns left to cross the stream (or dry river bed) but we keep straight ahead, still climbing.

We soon emerge at the top of the woods, with open fields on both sides, but we are still following a stony track, with ramsons alongside. The track narrows as we walk between hedges, and where there are stiles on left and right, we turn right over the stile to cross a small field to another stile and out on to the narrow road. Here is a seat for rest or picnic if required, before carrying straight on across the road. This seat, surrounded by daffodils and lesser celandine is a lovely memorial to Margaret Babington, situated in a peaceful location with wonderful views over the Wye Valley. We heard skylarks singing and saw a pair of long tailed tits gathering feathers for nesting material, whilst resting on this seat one day in early April (4).

Go over the stile, following the sign to Penterry Church, and walk along the right side of the field, with clear views to the two masts on Gaer Hill to our left. In the right corner of the field is a stile and gate, beyond which we head diagonally left towards the tiny stone church. The churchyard contains some quite recent graves, as well as magnificent trees including a yew and a wellingtonia. The grassy churchyard is made colourful by wild flowers, violets, daffodils and ladies smock.

Leave the south side of the churchyard through an iron gate, and head diagonally right to a large gate and out on to the narrow road, where we turn right. Wild flowers are bright and colourful alongside this lane. As we begin to descend, look for the clumps of small star shaped pink flower with shiny green leaves on the left, and then a cover of bluebells on the left. A footpath comes in from the left, another mass of bluebells is growing on the left, and then a track goes off to the right. We just continue along the road, through woodland carpeted with flowers and alive with bird noises. There were chiffchaffs singing and also a flock of fieldfares here when I last walked this way in mid-April 2000, giving a good indication of the change of seasons experienced in this month. Then we have another small hill to descend, between banks with wall pennywort amongst the variety of flowers – it is a real botanists' dream around here.

At the bottom of the hill, reach a small crossroads **(5)**, where we turn right along a bridleway signed to Tintern and Chapel Hill. Climb at first but the track splits after about 50 metres and we fork left. Climbing gradually, just before reaching some isolated houses and a scrap heap of old vehicles, go left off the track and follow a public bridleway near the edge of the woods. Once past the houses, the path begins to descend through the woods and emerges on to a broad stony forestry track, about 30-40 metres from a narrow road. Do not go to the road, but turn right along the track, signed towards Butcher's Grove and Church Grove, and leading gently uphill in Glyn Woods, passing the No Unauthorised Vehicles sign. Down to the left is the narrow Angidy Valley, centre of iron working in the past. We soon reach a point where a path comes in from the left. Shortly beyond this is a picnic table on the left and, after another 30 metres the track divides three ways, very sharp right, straight on or slightly left.

We go slightly left, towards Highfield House, and just by the gate posts, follow the right-hand drive for a few metres until we can move on to a narrow path between a low wall and small trees, to the right of this drive. This leads us past the buildings on our left, across a track going to houses on our right, but keeping straight ahead drop steeply down a narrow path to the stream. Turn left to walk down this small valley, beneath a wooden plank bridge and then immediately turn right to cross the stream and continue alongside the edge of the garden. The path goes into woods, with the stream now down to the left, and we reach a meeting point of several routes. Of the three possibilities going ahead, take the middle route, a narrow path between old banks. This descends slightly and leads through to a point where paths meet again, but we just keep straight ahead and soon can see the ruins of St Mary's church on our right. St Mary the Virgin was rebuilt in 1866 but was destroyed by fire in 1977. The burial ground has been associated with the Abbey since the 12th century.

Go over the stone stile into the churchyard, which gives us good views to the Abbey ruins. All over the churchyard as well as inside the remnants of the church, wild flowers are abundant – wood anemones, lady's smock, lesser celandine. Leave the churchyard by the iron gate at the downhill edge of churchyard. Pass the seat with good views over Tintern village and the Wye, and walk downhill, along the old steep cobbled track. When this reaches a narrow road, turn right, with a stone wall containing pennywort on our left, and retrace steps down to the main road and the Abbey.

A ruined wall in the abbey

May
Hay-on-Wye

The fascinating small market town of Hay-on-Wye is set in the heart of magnificent hilly countryside covered with fields, woods and hedges, overlooked by the dramatic hills of the Black Mountains. The town provides a starting point for a variety of walks to suit all tastes, if you can tear yourself away from the bookshops!

Lengths of walks: the main walk from Hay-on-Wye to Hay Common is 6½ miles (though with a shorter 4½ miles option if required) and the walk to Clyro is 4 miles. Time required is 3 hours and 2 hours respectively. The two can be combined, with a break for lunch in Hay.

Terrain: undulating, but with no very steep ascents or descents. Larger hills can be seen all around.

Maps:O.S. Outdoor Leisure 13, Brecon Beacons East, or Landranger 161.

Starting point: Hay-on-Wye GR229422, two miles off the A438 Hereford to Brecon road.

Public Transport: access by bus is possible from Hereford and Brecon.

Facilities: Tourist Information Centre in Hay-on-Wye (phone 01497 820144); there is a wide choice of refreshments in Hay and also the pub in Clyro.

Weather

May in 1999 was a warm month, though not very sunny, both of these facts being influenced by the frequency of southerly winds with cloudy skies. There were very few hot days over 20°C, but no really cold days either. The month was wetter than average though as some of the rain was in thunderstorms there were considerable localised variations. The old saying: *A May flood never did any good*, is certainly true, as it would be less expected at this time of year, and would damage the crops in the fields.

A bright and warm sunny weekend gave the month a good start over the Bank Holiday but low pressure dominated by the end of the first week. Cooler and showery weather was experienced in the Wye Valley and over much of England and Wales.

High pressure gave a few settled days in mid-month, though northerly winds kept temperatures low, from 17-20°C daily maxima, with slight frosts in the north. Although not very cold, we are always surprised by this cooler weather, which happens in most years. This cooler period nearly coincided with one of Buchan's spells of weather. He was a meticulous student of the weather during his lifetime (early 19th century), and he found that 9th-14th often experienced cool weather, though his readings and records were for Scotland. Thundery weather spread north from France on the 19th, and Atlantic fronts brought unsettled weather from 21st for a few days. The 25th is St Urban's day, noted as one of the old Days of Prediction used in Weather Lore, and was a day of cool showery weather though with sunny periods. Fortunately, these old Days of Prediction are not always correct. More thunderstorms came from the south on the 27th and again on the 29th there were heavy showers, with cooler weather bringing the month to a close.

The Countryside

If the month has been wet and warm, as this year, the countryside becomes very green and lush by the end of the month. Rapid growth

The countryside near Hay-on-Wye

produces mini jungles in hedgerows, along lanes and roadsides, in corners of gardens and any patches of waste ground. This is all very good for wild life, though can impede walking as footpaths become overgrown.

Even the later trees become fully green by the end of the month, and hedgerows are bulging out into fields and across paths. Many of the spring flowers are fading, but there is plenty of colour, with new blooms. Hawthorn blossom survives throughout the month and the candles stand proudly on the horse chestnut, both pink and white. Formerly often called Whitsuntide candles, there is no longer an official Whitsuntide, although the second of the month's bank holidays is an equivalent. Elderflowers are growing in the hedges and rowan flowers open up on the hillside trees. Many roadsides are white with hawthorn and cow parsley. Bluebells floor many of the woods in the Wye valley, and stitchwort, herb robert and wild roses are common.

Swifts will be heard screeching overhead, with house martins and swallows twittering. Chiffchaffs (my **bird of the month,** shown on the right) are singing non-stop, as they have been since their arrival in April, or even late March. Gilbert White wrote of the chiffchaff – *the uncrested wren.... it does only two piercing notes.* These tiny warblers fly from the Mediterranean lands to summer in Britain, and nest in dense vegetation such as nettles and brambles quite close to the ground. Chiffchaffs look very similar to willow warblers, though these birds winter in more tropical latitudes. Many other bird songs are evident in the hedgerows, though the dawn chorus lessens by the end of the month, as many birds are feeding young, which are calling plaintively for food. Some of these fledglings will soon have to fend for themselves, as parents begin their second brood. Warblers including the whitethroats are a little later than the resident birds, as mentioned by Browning in his 'Home thoughts from Abroad'.

And after April, when May follows,
And the whitethroat builds, and all the swallows.

Cereals are growing in a few of the fields, and lambs are now quite large. The first silage will have been cut. Around Hay-on-Wye most fields are in grass, but several fields of cereals are growing well. On a bright sunny day, the colour and freshness of the countryside is mainly green of hedges and fields, white of horse chestnut, hawthorn and cow parsley, and yellow of buttercups, dandelions and rape. As was said in *The Canterbury Tales*, 'He was as fresh as is the month of May'.

Hay-on-Wye

The name of this border town is derived from the Norman haie, a fenced or hedged enclosure, and Y Gelli, the Welsh name, means a grove. Known world-wide as 'The Town of Books', it contains over 30 book shops and a variety of other shops, and has been the home of a famous Literary Festival since 1988, generally at the end of May, and sponsored by the Sunday Times. A motte and bailey castle was built near St Mary's church about 1100, by the Norman Lord, Bernard Newmarch, and then a stone castle was built nearby about 100 years later, by William de Breos II. In its chequered history, it was destroyed by King John, fired by Prince Llewellyn, rebuilt by Henry III and restored to the de Breos family. Subsequently, it suffered more setbacks. It became the residence of Hay vicars in Victorian times, and is now owned by Richard Booth, and – needless to say – it is a book shop. The church of St Mary dates from the 12th century but only the lower part of the west tower remains from that time. Major changes in 1866 included the creation of three Gothic arches in the chancel and the addition of an apse. Hay has been a market town for several hundred years, still has a small cattle market, and is now an

St Mary's church

important tourist centre. Situated at the crossing point of the river, where there was a ford in the past, the first bridge was constructed in 1763, but was washed away in the huge floods of 1795. The present bridge dates from 1958. Surrounded by magnificent scenery in all directions, Hay is overlooked by Black Hill, 640 metres (2101ft) the highest summit in the southern half of England.

Clyro

The village is now bypassed by the A438 and preserves an air of peace and quiet. The name is derived from Clidderwy, meaning the River Wye flowing over a bed of clay. The settlement dates back to Roman times, when a large camp was set up at the site of Boatside Farm. The water for the village was supplied by seven springs until the mid-20th century but is now supplied by a reservoir at Penllan. One of the old taps has been preserved as a historical relic. The church of St Michael and All Angels dates back to the 12th century, but was rebuilt by Mr. J.A.T. Nicholson in 1853. Some of the grander pews have doors and are numbered. The church is built of grey stone with a few cut limestone and red sandstone pieces round windows and turrets. Tall yews line the path to the church door, and inside are memorials to Kilvert and Baskerville. The Kilvert Gallery is in Ashbrook House, and is where Robert Francis Kilvert (born 1840) lived as curate from 1865-72. He then returned to his native Wiltshire, but came back to live in Bredwardine (1877-79) where he is buried. His diaries of the daily happenings in the Wye Valley and in Wiltshire give a fascinating and detailed insight into life in the 1870s. The village is part of a large parish, and the ancient rhyme says: *Clifford, Clyro, Clodock and Clun, are the largest parishes under the sun.*

The Hay-on-Wye walk

We take in a little of the riverside path as well as climbing slightly to the edge of Hay Common in this 6½ mile walk. Start by turning left from the car park (1) and then first right (TURN LEFT here if the 4½ mile walk is preferred) along Castle Street, passing the old Fire Station which was Richard Booth's first book shop. Then, fork left to pass the old Spinning and Weaving mill on the right, and the Catholic church on the left. We pass the 1884 Clock Tower on the right, before turning left to the river and the bridge.

The path down to the river bank is on the right side of the road, but once down by the river turn left to walk upstream. There are two paths here, the slightly higher one being the line of the old railway which opened in 1864, linking Hereford to Hay and Brecon, built to replace a horse-drawn tramway, used for carrying coal from Brecon (and the Abergavenny and Brecon canal). Follow the tree lined path, named the Bailey Walk, after Sir Joseph Bailey who created this in 1884. Occasional views of the river can be seen through the trees, on our right, and on the left, we pass a stream and path coming in from the left, from near St Mary's church. Pass Warren Cottage, and go on through an iron kissing gate to emerge from the trees on to a large grassy area sloping down to the river. Keep on the left side of this popular playground and picnic area, The Warren, to an iron kissing gate; follow a narrow path through to a stile and out on to the narrow road, where we turn left.

Walk along this driveway, passing foundations of a former railway bridge and out to the road. Turn left to walk through an area of fairly new housing, passing the church, adjacent to which is a stream and footpath signed to the waterfall and the riverside path, where we were walking half an hour ago. Note the small market place, the former site for the tramway wharf, on the left before reaching the main road, where on our right is the Swan at Hay Hotel. Here we turn right to proceed on the 4½ mile walk south to the edge of Hay Common. (our car park is just a short distance to the left).

Keep ahead, with the Swan at Hay on our right and we are now on Church Street. Forest Road is to the left, and the sign straight ahead to Brecon 16 miles suddenly dropping to 15 after a few metres. Keep along this road as far as the Cemetery (2) on the left, where we turn, following the bridleway sign and walking alongside a small stream, Login Brook. A field on the right may have marquees, for the famous Hay Festival.

The path leads through a wood with a variety of trees, and the damp environment near the stream supports many ferns and a rich assortment of wild flowers. Cross footbridges and follow the stream as we gradually gain height. A rocky bed and small gorges are reached as we climb. Go through a gate and emerge from the narrow wooded valley into more open land. Bearing slightly right walk through the middle of the narrow field, and as it widens out veer left to the corner of the field. Here there is a right turn signed, which we ignore, as we continue straight ahead along the narrow path through trees and climbing. Emerge on to a patch of open common and stay close to the right margin. After a few more trees, when the path splits, we do not follow the hedge on the right this time. Instead, head diagonally left across the middle of the open common to the stile by the iron gate, at the top end of this field. Once over the stile, head diagonally right across the next field to a stile by a gate, and on across the next field, passing an old derelict building – The Werns – where jackdaws nest, on the right. You then reach a clear path leading through Wern Wood, still climbing slightly.

Once through this old wood, cross a short open area, and go through a few more trees to reach a stile. Beyond this, follow the left margin of the field for about 150 metres, as far as the gate where we turn left, along the remnants of an old track following a single line of trees. This track leads us through to a stile and gate, and out on to the narrow road, where we turn left **(3)**.

This banked lane is lined with wild flowers, including yellow archangel, stitchwort, a few bluebells and herb robert. Pass Pant-y-Fithel on the right, and shortly beyond this go right over a stile in the hedge, and immediately left over another stile to walk slightly downhill towards the far left corner of the field. Here at the stile, the path divides but we fork right to descend to the stile and footbridge over the stream to reach Wernwilk House. From the courtyard area in the middle of the buildings, go left along the driveway, with the stream across one field to our left. When the drive divides, go right to walk along to Dan-y-fforest and pass to the left of the buildings through a gate. After a few metres, go slightly right through the next gate and continue along the left margin of the field.

Go on through another gate and field, with good views to Cusop Hill up to the right, and over another stile to keep ahead, with the hedge now on our right, to reach the road. Turn left for about 100 metres along the road, then go right over a stile, to follow the acorn as we are now on Offa's Dyke Footpath **(4)**. Cross the field, passing an

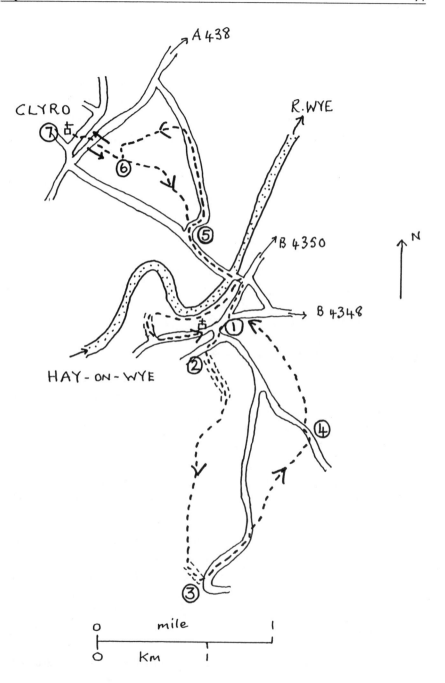

advert for Kilvert's Hotel and continue over a stile and downhill, with a wood containing a noisy rookery on our right. Cross a footbridge over a tributary stream, and walk on, with the small Dulas Brook to our right. This stream is the boundary between England and Wales at this point (We are in Wales). Hay-on-Wye is now in sight and we cross the fields to arrive back in the town, near the large car park, the castle and the Tourist Information Centre.

The Walk to Clyro

From the car park (1) in the centre of Hay-on-Wye, walk straight across the road and along Back Fold, through to Castle Street where we turn right passing shops and then the old castle, now a book shop. Pass to the right of the Old Town Hall, where there is a plaque on the wall, and turn left between the Town Hall and the Butter Market. Turn right along the front of the Old Butter Market, rebuilt in 1833, and passing more shops (Antique Market) continue nearly as far as the Kilvert Hotel. Turn left and go down St John's Place, turn left at the cross roads to walk to the Clock Tower. Turn right here and then left to follow the road towards Clyro.

This leads us down towards the river, and on the right is the way down to the riverside path (followed in the walk to The Warren). Cross the bridge and just beyond the river is the sign for Offa's Dyke Path, which we are not following. Walk on along the pavement, noting the old Radnorshire milepost on the other side of the road. Climb steadily, with colourful flowers brightening up the verge – broom, daisies and wild roses. The path is lined by small rocks of igneous origin, some of which may be showing flakes of mica, glinting in the sun.

At the top of the hill, turn right (5) along a minor road, and to the left is the driveway into the Radnors End camp site, and our return route will join the road here. For the outward journey continue along the road, passing a fairly new house on the left, and when the road bends left, admire the views to the right, over Hay-on-Wye. There is another house to the left here, but on the right are the large buildings of Boatside Farm, and here is the site of a large Roman encampment, though little evidence remains. It was located on the route from

Brecon to Kenchester (near Hereford) and was large enough to accommodate a legion.

We walk along this narrow lane, for half a mile or so between flowery banks and thick hedges. It has been a tradition for Radnorshire farmers to use thick hedges to prevent stock escaping – and they are very good for wild life too. Pass the entrance to Tir Mynach, used by members of the Caravan Club, and then on the right is Boatside Cottage. The lane has grass in the middle by now, and after a further 200-300 metres the road begins to descend, and on the left is a gate, a stile and a footpath sign. Go left here and cross the field. Stay on the higher part of the field at first, but then descend slightly to the right, towards a damp marshy patch, to pass between gate posts (but no gate) and continue across the next field to a stile. Turn slightly right here, but follow the fence around the field margin, with another damp patch to our right, and Clyro Brook just beyond. Continue beyond the next stile and reach the old building of Clyro Mill (work was in progress to renovate, when last visited, in 2000). Our route ahead is really straight on alongside the driveway and field boundary, but the right of way makes a strange detour here. We have to turn left into the middle of the field, for about 200 metres to reach a cross path **(6)**, just before reaching a fence. If we turned left, this would lead us back to Hay-on-Wye and is the route of our return, but first we must visit Clyro. So, we will return to this point later, and our path ahead is to the right, aiming for the gate and stile, which can be seen on the field margin, alongside the driveway leading to and from the mill.

Once out of the field and on to the driveway, a few metres further will lead us to the main road, which bypasses the village. Cross the road and a narrow path leads to the village **(7)**, with the village pub and the Kilvert gallery on the right, the Post Office on the left, and the church across the road. The pub is the Baskerville Arms, formerly named the Swan Inn, and it takes its name from the Baskerville Family who lived at Clyro Court half a mile to the south. It is believed that Sir Arthur Conan Doyle based some of his famous story on this family and their dogs, but changed the location of the novel at the request of the family, to ensure their privacy was not disturbed.

After exploring the village, walk a few metres along the B4351 signposted to Hay-on-Wye, passing the new housing area on the left to reach the wooded mound, which is the site of Clyro Castle. The footpath alongside the road leads all the way back into Hay and can be used for the return walk. It passes through beautiful countryside with remarkable views ahead and slightly right to the Black Mountains, and further right to the Brecon Beacons.

An alternative, and even more rural route, is to retrace steps across the field near the old mill. Continue across this field **(6)**, rather than turning left to the mill, and follow the field boundary. After a few metres alongside the fence, keep straight ahead across the field to the hedge with a stile in a corner. Once over the stile turn left alongside the hedge, and after passing a metal gate on the left head slightly right across the field, to a stile by a gate. Over to the right are wonderful views towards the Brecon Beacons, and on the right at the foot of a large wood can be seen the buildings of Clyro Court. Continue straight ahead across the next field and at the hedge turn right for 30-40 metres to reach a gate and a stile. Turn left over a stile and cross a field, used as a caravan site, up the slope to reach a stile. Beyond this stile head diagonally right to a lone tree at the far corner of the field and on the top of this small hill. Leave the field over the stile and turn right along the field boundary, noting over to the left, the large complex of Boatside Farm and nearer is the more modern brick house seen earlier. Continue over the stile by the gate and along the driveway, with the camping field on the left, to reach the road, B4351 **(5)**. Turn left here to walk back into Hay-on-Wye. Cross the river bridge and turn right towards the Clock Tower, adjacent to which is a sign for the old county of Brecon.

June

Symonds Yat

Walking in the Wye Valley where the river flows into the hard rocks of the Forest of Dean and then out again, reveals a wide range of magnificent scenery with flat river plains, steep wooded valley sides and dramatic vertical cliffs. New views are revealed at every turn, with the Yat Rock giving the most dramatic views of all, and the countryside is enhanced by its wealth of natural history.

Lengths of walks: the Symonds Yat walk is 6 miles, with a shorter version of 5 miles if required, and will take 3-4 hours. The Goodrich walk is nearly 7 miles requiring 3-4 hours. The two walks can be linked together (by one mile each way along the river bank) to give a long walk of 15 miles.

Terrain: flat when close to the river, but the river valley sides are very steep, and have to be climbed twice in the Symonds Yat walk. The walk from Goodrich has the climb up on to Coppett Hill but otherwise is gentle. Both walks are likely to encounter some wet patches, unless the weather has been very dry.

Map: O.S. Outdoor Leisure 14, Wye Valley and Forest of Dean, or Landranger 162, Gloucester and Forest of Dean

Starting point: in the small car park at GR566157 reached from the A40 and then along the B4229 and the narrow road leading south from Huntsham Bridge. There is a larger car park on the other side of the road GR 564155. Both of these car parks can also be reached along the B4432 from Coleford. Goodrich is reached from the A40, along the B4229.

Public Transport: buses from Ross-on-Wye, Gloucester and Monmouth pass Goodrich.

Facilities: the nearest town is Monmouth, which has a TIC (phone 01600 713899) and there is also a Tourist Information Centre in Coleford (01594 812388). Refreshments are available in Symonds Yat East, Goodrich and at Yat Rock.

Weather

Often a sunny and warm month, June generally produces a mixed bag of weather conditions, but length of daylight makes this a good month for long walks. In 1999, there was no prolonged hot spell, and monthly temperatures were below average. On the other hand, the rainfall was above average, and associated with some humid southerly air from Spain and France, several rainy days were quite thundery. Because of this, rainy periods were often short and sunshine totals were quite high. The month started with high pressure for a few days and then low pressure took over, giving a few days of northerly weather when daily maxima rarely exceeded 20°C. Pressure rose again at the end of the second week, for a sunny spell of clear days and cool nights. There were a few ground frosts recorded in the Scottish glens, but pleasantly warm afternoons were experienced over much of England.

"*Summer afternoons, summer afternoons; to me those have always been the two most beautiful words in the English language*" – said Henry James in "Backward Glance."

The month ended with another spell of Atlantic weather. Called the midsummer month, this is often a misnomer for June, as in many years the summer has hardly started. The 11th June is St Barnabas, and before the calendar change of 1752, this was the longest day, and is still said to be the day when the first harvest of hay should be cut. '*In the hay season when there is no dew, it indicates rain*' often turns out to be a good forecast.

The Countryside

June is burstin' out all over (Oscar Hammerstein II) is true every year, whatever the weather, as growth of plants is rapid throughout the month. The countryside was looking very green throughout the month, though still with occasional yellow fields of rape and the early flowering on isolated blue fields of flax. Grass for silage was being cut in several fields, and cereals crops were up to full height but not turning yellow. Early in the month, many birds were still singing, often hidden in the foliage, although a few species are kind enough to sing from bush tops so that we could see them.

By the end of the month many families of birds were in evidence, with little fluffy tits with short tails, many sparrows and other finches shuffling their wings in eager anticipation of food, and calling hopefully whenever parents appeared in sight. Most obvious perhaps were the families of starlings, with the two adults followed by three or four brown young, always hungry. If parents started on a second brood, the first generation quickly had to learn how to find food for themselves. Some birds still manage to fit in a little singing each day, in spite of searching for food. This can be very hard work, as it is known that swallows and other insect-eaters, may complete over 300 sorties per day to carry food to the nestlings. Swallows and house martins will be twittering, and swifts will be screeching overhead, and in the evenings, in addition to the birds the bats will also be busy collecting insects. Insect numbers are increasing, which is good for the birds but not so good for the walkers – especially on the more humid days. Butterflies add colour to sunny days, and may be seen dancing in the sunshine in the woodland glades.

The grass begins to go brown in June in dry hot years, but not in 1999 (or 2000). Roadside verges and hedgerows are prolific with wild flowers, and each week sees a change in this profusion. It certainly will be a colourful month whatever the weather, with a lot of red, mauve and purple this month, taking over from the dominant white of last month, with horse chestnut and hawthorn.

Our **bird of the month** is the peregrine falcon, which has had an upsurge in numbers, after a serious decline in the 1950s and 1960s. Nationally the peregrine became extinct over much of its range, but fortunately has become a real success story in the last 20-30 years. Peregrines nested on the cliffs of Coldwell Rocks for decades, until the 1950s, but they returned in the 1980s and have nested here ever since. The RSPB has provided wardens to watch over the nest as well as to inform visitors about the birds. Nothing is more dramatic or exciting than seeing one of these birds in a high-speed dive to catch their prey – often pigeons.

Peregrine falcon

Symonds Yat

The settlements take their name from Mr. Symonds, a former High Sheriff of Herefordshire who owned much of the land around here in the 17th century. Yat means a gate or a pass, which seems appropriate for the impressive landscape seen here in the Wye Valley. Symonds Yat has a large car park on the west of the narrow road, near to the toilets, snack bar and information centre, and alongside the wooden footbridge, which leads over the road to Yat Rock. From this famous viewpoint, at the top of the 120 metres (400ft) cliff, are great views along the river and a clear telescopic view to the Coldwell Rocks where the peregrine falcons nest. Jackdaws and a pair of ravens nest nearby, with buzzards nesting in the woods across the river. Near the car park is the site of an Iron Age fort, dated to about 2000 years ago. This can be seen in the embankments between the main car park and the Information Centre.

The River Wye

The river follows a very peculiar route, the result of its history and the course selected by the river thousands of years ago, when it was flowing at the height level with the top of the valley. It has cut down

The ferry to Symonds Yat

into the rocks to flow at its present level. Coming from the Goodrich direction the river flows into the hard rocks of the Forest of Dean just south of the castle, then flows north out of the Forest of Dean to Huntsham Bridge before going south and back into the harder rocks between Symonds Yat East and West. The deeply cut meander is called an incised meander and is the result of superimposed drainage, which means that the course followed by the river was determined at a much higher level, at the top of the present valley. The river has cut steeply down, when it had extra powers of erosion, perhaps from meltwater during the Ice Age.

Goodrich Castle

The earliest record of Godric's Castle is 1102, though nothing remains from that time. The oldest part is the square Norman keep from the mid-12th century. The castle was constructed by the feuding Marcher lords, to control the river crossing, and was one of the last castles to surrender to Oliver Cromwell during the Civil War in the 1640s. The castle was badly damaged by 'Roaring Meg' a massive mortar which can be seen in the Churchill Gardens museum in Hereford. The impressive moat shows exposures of the underlying red

Goodrich Castle

rock on which it was built. The church of St Giles dates from the 13th century but with later changes. The village of Goodrich is close to the castle and contains several sandstone buildings, and several Gothic buildings too.

The Symonds Yat Walk

Start from the small car park (1) near the Symonds Yat Viewpoint on the left side of the road, opposite the old Post Office, about 100 metres after passing beneath the wooden footbridge. This is reached by driving south from Huntsham Bridge along the narrow road which turns off the B4229. This circuit is about 6 miles, but a slightly shorter route is also possible if required, which will cut out one of the steep climbs referred to in this account.

Walk south-east from the car park, following the footpath into the woods. This leads slightly downhill along a fairly straight path, with an open field visible a few metres to the right, and a fence guarding the steep slope on the left. Ramsons are numerous along here, and the blue of bugle can be seen in the grassy verges. Birds will be singing to us as we continue along the narrow path, which can be muddy in places. The muddiest spots are when we reach a small cross stream, which is where the clays of the Coal Measure rocks rest on top of the Carboniferous limestone which is responsible for the formation of steep cliffs to our left. After the stream, we bend left, still following a clear path. The path splits and we take the right fork, going slightly uphill. You may be able to see a stile on the edge of the woods up to the right, and our onward route could go over there, across a narrow field and turn left along the driveway, with the field margins on our right. This will lead along to the left of Bicknor Court and Farm. If this stile is still not usable, stay in the woods and follow the path (right fork) as it leads along the top of the steep slope down to our left. At a gap in the woods where we reach a fence, and a stony track going steeply down to the left, we go over the fence, and immediately turn right to the gate. Once over or through the gate, head diagonally left across the field to a stile in the corner of the field. This is the place you will reach if you have followed the track and field margin just mentioned earlier.

Go over the stile, and across a small field to a gate, then diagonally right to another small gate and across another small field to a gate, and walk along a grassy patch between fences, to a stile and the woods. Whilst crossing these paddocks the farm buildings have just been a few metres to our right.

The path leads through a small wood and out to a narrow road (2) where we turn left. Follow this narrow lane between flower covered banks, to pass the house named Rosemary Topping, and when the road ends at a few houses, two tracks continue. Take the left fork into the woods, to reach a gate and a stile, beyond which we continue still following a track, with woods to our right. Passing the end of the woods, the views open up to the river, and also straight ahead to the vertical outcrops of limestone, the Coldwell Rocks. There may be deer in the fields around here, and you should look for buzzards floating overhead. The track soon bends right, to descend to an old stone barn, but we keep straight ahead along the path leading into the woods.

The broad track leads through the woods and we come down to the river bank. Turn left here, over a stile, and we have now joined the Wye Valley Walk – a gravelled path here. This follows the route of an old railway, the Ross-Monmouth line which opened in 1873, but was closed by the Beeching changes in 1965. Reach a gate and a stile, and the car park where we began this walk, is up to the left, about nearly 120 metres (400ft).

At an open patch the boarded up entrance to the tunnel can be seen to our left, and up above this is an isolated house. We join another track coming from the left, the driveway to the house, and begin to climb slightly. The path soon splits with the forest track going straight ahead, signposted to the Yat Rock, and the Wye Valley Walk going right.

Fork right, down stone steps and then a few wooden steps, which all can be muddy and slippery after wet weather, to drop down to the river plain, here at about 25 metres above sea level (80ft). Very lush vegetation thrives here, with particularly fine nettles, flowers, and a variety of trees of varying size. Across the river is a grassy meadow (visited in the Goodrich Walk) sloping up gently whereas on our side is a wood on a very steep slope. We reach a tidy garden and a small house set a few metres back, presumably to get above flood level, and begin to move away from the river here, climbing a little. The path splits **(3)** and we take the left fork, unless we are intending to walk along the river bank, to Huntsham Bridge **(7)** more than a mile away, to link up with the Goodrich Walk.

We take the left fork, which climbs quite steadily away from the river, up some wooden steps, where we are on the Wye Valley walk and also the Wye Valley Farm Park Walk. Pass a few lumps of Quartz Conglomerate rock (see Introduction – page 5), with clearly visible white pebbles of quartz, similar to the conglomerate seen on the climb up to the Kymin, only a few miles downstream. Also notice the conglomerate used, with other rocks, in the walls of the old ruined building passed on our left. If getting breathless climbing up the slope, pause, and admire some lovely ferns including harts tongue on this stretch of the walk.

We are now beginning to bend round the end of Huntsham Hill, and views open up to our right along the valley, with the spire of Goodrich church being prominent. The path splits and the Wye Valley Walk goes left up some new wooden steps, and the Wye Valley Farm Park Walk goes right. We go left, and climb to a broad track where we turn right, and up to our left can be seen a large outcrop of conglomerate. The broad track passes through an assortment of deciduous trees, and then begins to descend slightly. Look for a narrow path going off to the left, the Wye Valley Walk, which we follow, and pass the edge of a dark coniferous wood sloping up to our left. The main path keeps fairly level but at the end of the coniferous stretch of trees on our left, there is a narrow path going up slightly higher in the wood, and at first it follows an old sunken track **(4)**.

For a **Short Cut** return to our starting point, saving about one mile, and cutting out the very steep climb up from the river bank, go left along this path. It climbs gradually, with rocky outcrops overhanging on our left. Wild flowers notably bluebells line much of the floor, as we walk on to a small gate at the edge of the wood. Keep straight ahead, near the right margin of an open field, from where there are good views over to the right, to houses perched on the steep slope. Ahead can be seen the wooded slopes on both sides of the river, and some rocky outcrops showing through gaps in the trees. Across the field we reach a gate and proceed along a path through more woodland. The road is visible just down to our right. Our path is joined by a larger path coming in from our left, and becomes a broad track soon to reach a small (private) parking area, alongside the road. We turn left here, but take care as the road is very narrow in places, and is often busy. Pass the Symonds Yat Baptist Chapel on

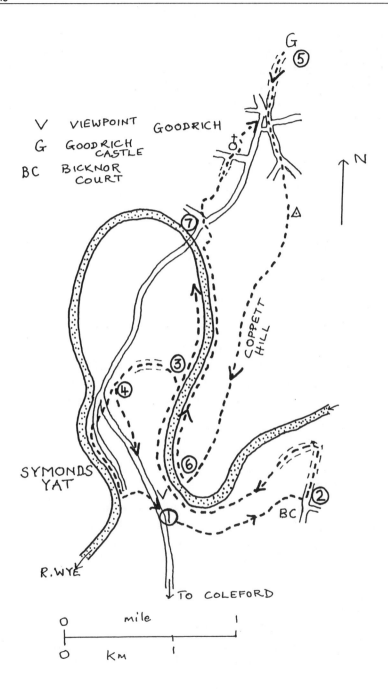

V VIEWPOINT
G GOODRICH CASTLE
BC BICKNOR COURT

GOODRICH

N

COPPETT HILL

SYMONDS YAT

R. WYE

TO COLEFORD

0   mile   1

0   Km   1

our left, then a house offering B and B on the right. After another house on the left is a footpath signed to Ross and Welsh Bicknor, but we stay on the road, climbing steadily. Pass a wide forest track on the right, the Old School House on the left, and walk on beneath the wooden footbridge, which leads to the Viewpoint, where telescopes will be trained on the peregrines' nest. A further 150 metres or so will take us back to the starting point.

Main Walk, continued.

Where the two paths mentioned above diverge, looking down to the right at this point can just be seen the end of the track we were walking along a few minutes ago, at the point where it reaches the road. Here there is a turning space for buses, which are not allowed to proceed further along the narrow road.

For the full six miles walk, including another steep climb, continue along the main path, the Wye Valley Walk, and this passes more conglomerate outcrops and soon slopes gently down to the road. Turn left for about 60 metres of brisk walking, as this road is very narrow and often busy. At the passing place on the right side, the onward W.V.W. path goes back into the woods, and descends quite steadily down the valley side – with more large rocky outcrops on the left. Houses will be visible on the opposite valley side, to our right. We descend to another narrow road, and turn left here, for about 30 metres, then go right, on a grassy path through the middle of a field (onions, in the year 2000), across to the river bank and the site of a ferry (adults 60p in 2000!) across to Symonds Yat West, and Ye Olde Ferrie Inne.

Turn left along the river bank to reach the settlement of Symonds Yat East, with small camping site, car parking, a ferry, canoe hire, pub, hotel and tea shop. The last buildings are two hotels and, although the Wye Valley Walk continues along the river bank, our path turns left here, signposted away from the river (Yat Rock ½ mile), to pass between the Royal Hotel (an old railway station is in the grounds of the Royal) and the Forest View Hotel, along a narrow path between wall and fence. We climb steeply through the woods, with limited views except in winter. Just before reaching a forest track, turn right at the sign to Symonds Yat Rock, along a permissive path with new wooden steps, which continues the steep ascent. Cross a track but keep climbing, and just before the top, the path divides, left to Welsh Bicknor and Ross, and right to Yat Rock.

We turn right, passing a spot with a clear view back down to the river at Symonds Yat, and emerge by the Information Centre. Cross the wooden footbridge to visit the Yat Rock, to admire the wonderful views along the Wye Valley, and also possibly to see a peregrine falcon. Only then should you return to your car, having seen one of the finest views in the United Kingdom!

The Goodrich Walk

Starting point is at the picnic site **(5)** of Goodrich Castle, GR575196, reached on the B4234 from Ross-on-Wye, or any of three turnings off the A40. Length of walk is nearly 7 miles.

Walk from the castle back into the village, and close to the Post Office turn left, following the signpost to the Youth Hostel 1½ mls, Courtfield and Welsh Bicknor. Soon start climbing, pass a few houses and then the Dry Arch, a high bridge over a road B4229 to Kerne Bridge. Views to the left reveal Kerne Bridge, and towards the north-east can be seen the small church at Walford, and Chase Hill and the spire of Ross church. To the right are good views of Goodrich church, which we shall walk past later. When the narrow road divides, we keep straight ahead between the two roads beyond the triangle of grass, to climb up the steps and steep path towards Coppett Hill. The path leads up between large lumps of sandstone containing pebbles of quartz. This is the Quartz Conglomerate, which can be seen in other places along the Wye Valley. Just beyond one large rock to the right of the path, look out for a patch of wall pennywort growing on the left. Still climbing, we reach a path going down to the right, but we keep left, to reach a fairly horizontal cross path where we turn right. We are still in the woods, but soon emerge, with bracken on our right and views to the right. When the trees end on our left, and we are on the open common, views also open up to the left. Wild flowers and bird life are abundant, as we reach the tri-angulation point 188m (616ft), and beyond this at the highest point is the 18th-century Folly, an old ruined cottage.

We now follow a fairly level path through the bracken, and keep straight ahead, ignoring a cross-paths where a clear path goes sharp right. Bird life is varied, including blackcap, willow warbler, whitethroat, linnet, yellowhammer and hovering kestrel, and on my last walk along this path I was lucky enough to see a stoat crossing the path. A wall can be seen a few metres to our left, and after about a mile as we begin to descend we enter a shrubby and then a wooded area, which clothes the southern end of this hill. We descend steadily, knowing that when we emerge at the bottom, the Coldwell Rocks and the peregrine nest will be on the other side of the valley. Go over the stile, to leave the woods, and enter a rich lush buttercup meadow which we cross to the river bank **(6)**. The peregrine nest is slightly to the left, up on the vertical limestone walls, as we turn right to walk alongside the river, heading downstream (northwards).

Notice a house on the left, near where the old railway line enters a tunnel, then go over a stile, where an old building (Hentland) is up to our right. Then notice a second house on the other side of the river, and shortly beyond that the woods on other bank end, to reveal open fields of farmland. The woods on our right gradually approach the river bank, and are probably lined with masses of foxgloves in June. We reach a gate and stile and continue along a track, which has come down from the right, out of the trees and foxgloves. The track runs alongside the river bank for 200 to 300 metres, passing a slightly turbulent stretch of water, to reach another gate and stile, where the track veers slightly right away from the river, but we follow the path along the river bank. The buildings of Mainoaks are across to the right, as we continue for another quarter mile to a stile beyond which we follow a narrow path and then bend right to pass Ferry Cottage, turn left along the drive and walk out to the road. A few metres to the left is Huntsham Bridge **(7)**, and just beyond the bridge is the riverside path on the other bank, which is the route to link with the Symonds Yat walk if required (an additional 7 or 8 miles).

However for our onward walk turn right to follow the road up to the T-junction, where the driveway from Mainoaks and Rocklands reaches the road. Go straight across the road, over a stile and along a narrow path for 30 metres, then left over another stile. Our onward route could then be turning right to follow the hedge up the right side of the field and through into the next field, but we are arrowed to go along the left margin of the field for 40 metres and then head right, across the middle of the field to a stile on the right side of the Sewage Works. Beyond this stile the arrow points left along the field margin, passing a small wood and then heading across the field to the right corner by a house. At this point turn sharp right to walk back along the margin of the same field with the hedge on our left, to the cross paths at the end of the field, where we would turn left. That seemed a long triangular way round this field, but the same point can be reached more easily by turning right from the stile by the Sewage Works, and following the hedge and then turning left at the end of the field, still following the field boundary with a hedge on the right, to reach the same cross paths. Go straight on here, with a hedge on the right and an open field to our left.

At the end of the field go over the stile and turn left, and the path becomes a track leading out to a narrow road, where we turn right. On the house to our right, Granton House, is a memorial plaque to Joshua Cristall (1768-1847) the watercolour artist who lived here from 1823-1841. On the left is the Old Vicarage, and then we turn left through the gate along a grassy track leading to the church. The lovely stone church has a graceful spire, and notice the conglomerate rocks used in the walls. House martins nest near the church door. In the bottom corner of the churchyard is an old iron kissing gate, and we walk on through there, alongside a field margin to another kissing gate, and then on the path leading down alongside the new school (building in progress June 2000). Turn left along the road, walking towards the Post Office, and at the junction of the roads, fork right towards Goodrich Castle.

July
Plynlimon

Plynlimon is a huge though not rugged mountain, and the wild and open hillsides are cut by deep and sheltered valleys. The moorland Wye soon gathers water from numerous tributaries and becomes a rocky bedded tumbling stream. After its confluence with the Tarenig, the valley widens and the landscape opens up slightly though many hillsides here are covered with plantations. Our walks along the valley only have gentle ascents but there are many steeper hills around for more energetic walking – across to the Severn valley perhaps!

Lengths of walks: 5 miles up towards the source – a linear walk there and back, and 3 miles for a circular walk downstream from the main road. The walk upstream could take 2-3 hours and a further 1 hour for the downstream circuit.

Terrain: high all around, though the walking remains in the valley, along clear and broad tracks and paths. The surrounding hills are extensive and several long routes across to the Severn valley or to the summit of Plynlimon are available for the more energetic. This is quite a wet area and so be prepared for rain, but in clear weather the views all around are magnificent across miles of wild moorland.

Maps: O.S. Landranger 136 and Explorer 214 cover the area of the walks.

Starting point: the Spring Lamb Farm, Pont Rhydgaled, at GR 840827, along the main road A44 between Llangurig and Aberystwyth. Parking is possible (permission must be sought first) just off this main road.

Facilities: nearest town is Llangurig, with a limited choice of refreshments, and the nearest Tourist Information Centres are in Llanidloes (01686 412605) and Rhayader (01597 810591).

Weather

Generally a warm month, and certainly a time of long hours of daylight, the weather can occasionally bring a few surprises, especially on Plynlimon, where rapid changes can bring cool conditions even in mid-summer. Generally however, rapid growth of plants continues, though at a slower pace than in May or June, and wet and dry spells will determine how the colour of the countryside changes. An old Monmouthshire saying suggests that the period from 4th-16th July is crucial to set the pattern for the rest of the summer: *If it is fine and summery, the rest of the summer is likely to be fine* – though British weather is never as straightforward as this suggests. The month does contain one of Buchan's spells, as he found that 12th-15th July was often a warm spell. In 1999, the month was sunny and warm with temperatures above average, and it was the sunniest July for about 15 years in many locations. There was no prolonged sunny spell, but a few periods with 2-3 warm days. One of these was accompanied by easterly winds when the high pressure moved over the North Sea, and during that time the west of Britain was warmer than the east, and temperatures around the Wye Valley were up to 28°C. There was a shortage of rain for the farmers, as this was the driest July since 1990. Much of the rain that did fall came in a few thundery outbursts, and some of these were accompanied by hail. A few small tornadoes developed in the Midlands, one in Selly Oak, Birmingham, causing considerable damage. The month ended with a very hot spell which became very humid – and thundery weather brought welcome rain to farms and gardens.

The Countryside

The lowland landscape looked very green at the beginning of the month, though the patchwork pattern of fields was showing several variations of colour. A few fields of hay have been cut, as well as one or two of the scattered fields of crops. On the hillsides are forests and woods, including large expanses of conifers but also small areas of mixed woodland. The wild grasses are going brown as they do, and on many of the lower hillsides there is good grass for grazing, though much of Plynlimon is covered by bracken and damp loving plants.

Not many butterflies have been seen this summer so far, but there was a steady increase in the second half of the month, and they were becoming quite numerous in the hot spell towards the end of July. Sun shining in the late evenings also shows up the increasing numbers of moths.

Bird song has steadily lessened as territorial claims diminish, and in the valleys the warblers have almost disappeared as they have gone silent and invisible in all the greenery. Many families of birds hunt for food together, twittering to each other as they do the rounds, looking for food, which is easily found at this time of year. Flocks of tits go from tree to tree, often with several different varieties of birds moving on together. Blackbirds and other thrushes are busy eating the fruits and berries in the hedges, and the blackbirds leave the worms in peace at this season as other foods are so plentiful. The larger birds such as crows or buzzards are still in family groups though soon the parents may drive the new generation away. Swallows and martins are twittering overhead, though the screaming of the swifts may have diminished. On the hills, larger birds include the crows and ravens, as well as buzzards, red kites and kestrels. The **bird of the month** is the much smaller meadow pipit, widely seen and heard on the slopes of Plynlimon. A little brown bird with a thin squeaky call as it flies away, is how the meadow pipit is regularly seen, but at close quarters it can show off its smart speckled breast and a patterned brown back. They carefully conceal their nest in clumps of grass but are vulnerable to ground feeding animals and always in danger from predatory birds. They are often the only small birds to be seen in hill country, and they mostly move down to lowlands for the winter. Wild flowers line the roads and the track along which we walk. Thistles are growing well, still with some lovely purple flowers as well as fluffy tops and seeds floating away, by the end of the month.

Meadow pipits

> Cut thistles in May, they grow in a day;
> Cut thistles in June, that is too soon;
> Cut them in July, then they die.

Llangurig

This small village was founded by Curig, a monk. It has a pub and an interesting Craft Shop. The church is on the site of the 6th-century Celtic church. It has a low and massive Radnorshire tower, and Sir Gilbert Scott added the shingle spire in 1877.

Pumlumon

Plynlimon is the anglicised version of this massive hill which has five summits and is the highest mountain of mid-Wales, reaching 752m (2468ft). Wide-ranging views are to be seen in all directions. It is the source of the three rivers, Severn, Wye and Rheidol. The Wye and Severn rise just two miles apart, and then meet up again at the Severn bridge, after following their very different routes to the sea. Ancient Ordovician and Silurian rocks make up this large hill mass on which have formed the rugged moorlands with expansive areas of peat bog. Several locations have been important for mining in the past, with lead being important in the 19th century. The Wye Valley mines were most active from 1863-1885, and there were mines west of the Wye in operation from 1866-1895. The mining caused pollution in the river – which is now noted for being so clean. Bird life on the hill includes a few red grouse, peregrine, raven, meadow pipits, whinchat, wheatear and red kite.

River Wye

The source of the river is at a height of about 680-690 metres (2230-2260ft) and in the 5 miles down to Pont Rhydgaled it loses about half of that height. Where we start the walk at the farm is at about 318m (1043ft), and we ascend to about 385 metres (1262ft) where a fence bars our way. On Plynlimon, the Wye is a typical upland stream, with a rocky bed, being fed by many small tributaries tumbling down the adjacent hillsides. It retains this characteristic for a short distance after being joined by the Tarenig, but it is then becoming a bigger river. As it heads towards Llangurig the valley begins to widen, even though it does narrow in several places throughout the entire length, even as far down as Symonds Yat and near to Chepstow. As it grows on its downward journey there are numerous small tributaries but also several major additions of water, notably the Elan, after which the Wye looks like the real river to be seen for the rest of its journey to the sea.

Forest Enterprise

Hafren and Tarenig forests were first planted in the 1930s though many of the original trees have been cut down and removed. In the Concept Plan for future development, some forest products will still be harvested, but the importance of the landscape is now a major consideration as is the restoration of areas of ancient woodland. Forest Enterprise is restoring or creating wetland and streamside habitats and gives priority to archaeological features. Studies are being made on several species of animals and birds in an attempt to understand and encourage a variety of wild life. Walkers are welcome in the forest, but must always bear in mind that forestry work may result in paths being closed occasionally. Forest Enterprise will put up notices to inform visitors of any restrictions.

George Borrow

This great traveller and writer had a very inquiring mind and was interested in everybody and everything. He learned the Welsh language, and in 1854 went on a long planned tour of Wales. When standing on the top of Plynlimon he claims to have recited the words of Lewis Glyn Cothi:

> *From high Plynlimon's shaggy side*
> *Three streams in three directions glide;*
> *To thousands at their mouths who tarry*
> *Honey, gold and mead they carry.*

The Plynlimon Walk

Location is along the A44, nearly 5 miles west of Llangurig, and this is nearly 3 miles each way for a linear walk to enjoy the upper valley of the Wye in its moorland setting. Be prepared for harsh weather, even in summer, for this is a wild hill landscape, although the walk follows a clear track and therefore there is no danger of getting lost. Park, with permission, in the entrance to the farm, or across the road in a small Forest Enterprise area (1).

A bridleway sign points us between the farm buildings, and we follow the arrow with the horseshoe, along the stony track which is now used for Rallying – an unusual form of farm diversification. The track was originally the route used by miners. The Wye (Gwy) is to our right, with clumps of trees down in the valley and in patches on the valley wall. In the variety of trees are a few lovely rowan, with berries just forming but becoming a riot of red in the autumn. A few small patches of coniferous woodland are to be seen, one containing pheasant breeding pens, and on the opposite side of the valley a couple of fenced fields show evidence of improved grassland. Generally, the areas of grassland around here are poor, with shallow soils and an unfavourable climate. A few wild flowers grow alongside the path and there are patches of grassy grazing for the sheep, though also bracken patches and some damp with marshy vegetation. Peat forms readily on the acidic rocks and with an annual rainfall of about 80 inches.

A heron was standing patiently in the stream the last time I walked here, and grey and pied wagtails are likely to be seen, and perhaps a goosander on the river. Meadow pipits are numerous all around. We cross over a bridge and the Wye, now on our left, is a delightful tumbling stream flowing over a rocky bed. As the track bends to the right, look for finches in the conifers, and note the rowan and gorse which add colour to the generally green or brown landscape. A few early signs of heather, and also areas of whinberry are to be seen as we pass a small weather station. There are several recording locations on Plynlimon, for study and research, and one of the many subjects to investigate is the difference between the Severn valley, which is largely forested, and the Wye, which is largely open moorland. How does this affect the total amounts of rainfall and the rates of throughflow? The studies have been conducted by the national Centre for Ecology and Hydrology.

We follow the stony track, ignoring the left turn over a ford, and continue to a group of farm buildings and an area with remnants of old mines and quarries. At the buildings are gates but we just keep straight ahead, to reach an open space, the site of old mining operations perhaps and now the location of a small track for the rally cars. A ford and bridge cross the stream here, but we keep ahead, and at the end of the open patch, by a few more old buildings, with barns holding the winter feed, the bridleway divides and we fork left, still following the horseshoe sign.

Pass through a gate and climb slightly, noting that the Wye is now turning away to our left. Go through a gate beyond the buildings and soon the track divides **(2)**. Do not follow the sign of the horseshoe, but fork left to walk to a small weather station and a flume on the Wye, which is as far as we can walk at present. No path continues up to the source of the Wye, which is only a small boggy patch. The moorland all around here is the home of a variety of upland plants and birds, sharing the hillside with the sheep, closely followed by

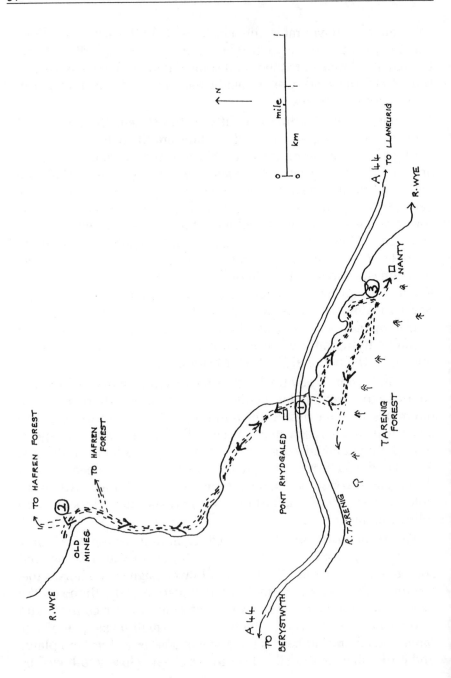

their lambs at this time of year. Black Highland cattle may also be seen on the hills. For a much longer walk it is possible to continue along the track marked with the horseshoe, into the Hafren forest and on to the source of the Severn.

We have climbed gently from a height of 318m (1043ft) by the road, to about 380 metres (1246ft) by the flume. The source of the Wye is about 2 miles further up the valley to the north-west, at a height of 680 metres (2230ft) in a narrow cleft on the hillside. We turn round and retrace our steps down the beautiful though often wild valley, noticing the large number of tributaries that may be cascading after heavy rain, which is not unusual here.

Downstream

Beyond the main road the Wye continues on its way to Llangurig, Rhayader and beyond. The stretch upstream from Rhayader is at present being waymarked to add to the existing official Wye Valley Walk from Rhayader down to Chepstow.

Cross the road (1) from the farm, and go through the Forest Enterprise Car park area and follow the surfaced road to a bridge. The footbridge and main bridge cross over the Afon Tarenig and a few metres to the left is its confluence with the Wye, which nearly doubles in size here. The Tarenig is generally very clear as it comes down the valley from the right. The enlarged river flows on eastwards over a gravelly bed which has been recently dredged in places.

Follow the gravel track into the forest, passing the Forest Enterprise notice welcoming walkers into the forest. Beware of forestry work, and also beware of Rally Cars on certain days each year. At the cross tracks turn left, following the arrow, and proceed along the level route through the trees. There are patches of undergrowth, with bracken and some mosses, and places where lichen is growing well on the trees. The trees are of mixed ages, though many areas are probably ready for cutting. Many bird noises will be heard in the forest, especially tits and goldcrests, but also a variety of finches, great spotted woodpeckers, wood warblers and, possibly, goshawk or red kite may be seen. Barn owls have returned to the Upper Wye valley, as a result of the efforts of the Powys Barn Owl Conservation Trust. Also in the woods can be seen several bat boxes, to provide shelter for the pipistrelles and Daubenton bats which feed along the Wye.

The track bends but just keep ahead, with the river a short distance to the left. The bed is rock and gravel, still looking like an upland stream, but the Wye is moving into a wider valley and beginning to lose its upland character, as it is no longer a mountain stream. Views open up downstream as our track begins to climb slightly and move away from the river. We rise up to reach a major horizontal track **(3)** where we turn right to complete this short circuit. For onward walking turn left here and after a short distance the track splits into three, with the left fork going down to Nanty and on downstream if following the Wye Valley Walk.

Having turned right, we just follow the broad and fairly horizontal track through the woods, listening to bird noises and looking at the variety of vegetation, mosses, lichen, some flowers, and patches of heather. When this track splits, near a shed, we turn right which leads us down to the cross track and straight on to the bridge over the Tarenig, and back to our starting point.

The upper Wye, as a small mountain stream

August

Mordiford and Fownhope

This fairly gentle walk across valleys and hills around the two picturesque villages of Mordiford and Fownhope passes through fields of varied crops and animals in the valleys of the Wye and its tributary the Lugg, where mixed farming is still practised in many of the small hedged fields.

Length of walk: 10 miles, with a short cut of 5½ miles. Time required is 5 hours, or 3 hours for the short cut.

Terrain: mostly gentle, with one steep climb on the Mordiford Loop. Several stiles, though not very high, are quite awkward.

Map: O.S. Explorer 189.

Starting point: can be in Mordiford (parking near the church or on the road to Hereford across the river bridge), in the car park at Swardon quarry (GR578385), but we are describing the walk as beginning from Fownhope church GR582343. This is reached along the B4224 from Hereford or along the narrow road leading from the A438 four miles east of Hereford.

Public Transport: a regular bus service runs to and from Hereford.

Facilities: nearest Tourist Information Centre is in Hereford (Phone 01432 268430). Refreshments available in the village pubs.

Weather

Generally a wet and warm month, August has been true to form this year, but with more rain than average over most of England and Wales, and some very heavy downpours associated with humid and thundery conditions. A very hot and humid start to the month was accompanied by thunderstorms, flooding and even a thunderbolt was recorded in Birmingham. At this time the night minima temperatures were often no lower than 14°C. By the end of the first week the weather was cooler but still showery though pressure built slightly around the time of the eclipse on the 11th, to give some sunshine in the Midlands and Welsh Borders, but not in Cornwall where the eclipse was total. Unsettled and showery weather soon resumed and small tornadoes were reported in several parts of England. A spell of fresher and quite sunny weather was experienced around the 21st-23rd, and then more heavy rain fell for a couple days on the

24th-25th. However, the month ended with a hot and dry spell, with pressure rising. Dew and damp spiders' webs were to be seen in the early mornings. An appropriate old rhyme for this month is:

> *The rain it raineth every day,*
> *Upon the just and unjust fellow;*
> *But more upon the just, because*
> *The unjust hath the just's umbrella.*

The Countryside

In mid-month the trees are still green but much darker than last month, although a few leaves are beginning to fade and fall. Seeds have fallen off the lime and other trees and a few early unripe conkers have fallen too. Rowan trees are covered with bright red berries. The elderberry bushes are prolific with fruit and many ripe blackberries provide tempting food for walkers as well as the birds and animals. The swifts have gone, but house martins and swallows are still to be seen, several pairs still visiting nests where the young are calling hungrily for yet more food. Mordiford church porch had a swallows' nest with young, and house martins were still nesting outside the village shop. This is a quiet month for birds, many of which are moulting. A few have already gathered into flocks, notably the noisy starlings, showing off their colourful winter plumage.

Lammas Day, 1st August, was traditionally the start of harvests, and August was generally regarded as an autumnal month. Nowadays it is very much considered as a summer month. A few of the cereal crops have been harvested, though others remain golden in the fields, perhaps delayed by the wet weather, although modern equipment can overcome many of the problems that farmers formerly found disastrous to their yields and income. Many of the fields in the Wye Valley are in grass anyway, and they are looking very green and lush, and some have already been visited by the muck spreader. Apple orchards may still be seen in the area visited in this month's walk, and there are a few hop fields in this area too, including smaller varieties not hung up on such tall poles as was traditional in the past. Hop bines are on sale, for use as floral decorations. Around Mordiford a real mixture of fields is to be seen, with hedges separating a wide range of land uses, showing some of the old traditions of mixed farming.

Hop field

Parts of the countryside are looking brown, not only where cereals have been harvested but also where wild grasses are growing and seeding, along field margins and in some meadows. Thistles have their fluffy tops, which are blown about in any gusts of wind, and butterflies are more numerous than earlier in the year, though not particularly so in this area. Flies however are very numerous and can become very annoying to walkers (and cattle and horses). In many ways August is not the best walking month even though it may be the warmest. Paths are often overgrown, brambles and nettles can be lethal and flies and wasps can be a nuisance. On a hot day, it is often interesting and pleasant to sit and watch, as nature will often come to you and show itself if you do not move. Take a leisurely picnic whilst out walking and you may see interesting bird and animal life. It is often thought that if you sit quietly for an hour or so, you will see more natural history than if out walking non-stop all day long. My **bird of the month** is the swallow, to be seen in several locations on this walk. Many pairs will have finished breeding and the adults will be preparing to set off on their migration, congregating on telegraph wires before departing. The young birds, recognis-

The easily-recognisable V-tailed swallow

able by their shorter tail feathers do not leave until later, having to find their own way to their winter homes in southern Africa. It takes them three months to reach Cape Town or Durban, and then they have to set off on the return journey in February, though this is quicker, taking about 40 days.

Haugh Wood

This mixed woodland was formerly owned by Hereford cathedral but is now managed by Forestry Enterprise. The strip along the road is owned by the National Trust and it contains wayfarer trees and other trees associated with ancient woodlands. Many paths meander through these woods and there is a clearly marked Forest Trail. The forest is located on a variety of rocks, with old Cambrian rocks outcropping at the top of the woods, and younger Silurian rocks forming the sloping land descending to the Wye Valley.

Fownhope

The ancient church of St Mary is 119ft in length, one of the longest in the county, and its square Norman tower dates from early 12th century. The spire was added in the 15th century and is covered by 22,000 oak shingles. Inside is a Norman tympanum showing the Virgin Mary holding baby Jesus. This was formerly over the door but was moved into the church for safer preservation. Nearby is the old parish chest – 9ft long and over 500 years old – made from a single oak tree. The stone lid of a 15th-century coffin is seen in the blocked up south doorway. The village stocks and whipping post are just outside the churchyard on the roadside, and nearby on the corner is

Norman tympanum

the carved sandstone mile stone, with very precise distances e.g. Hereford 6¼ miles and 56 yards, and Ross is 8¼ miles and 165 yards. The village still celebrates Oak Apple Day. The Green Man dates back to the end of the 15th century, the time of Henry VII. It was a coaching inn, and has enjoyed a varied history. One of its landlords was the prize fighter Tom Spring, heavyweight champion of England. Another of the early landlords commissioned the famous sign over the entrance to the Coaching yard.

You travel far, you travel near, its here you find the best of beer,
You pass the East, you pass the West, if you pass this you pass the Best.

The bark industry, lime kilns and milling were amongst the ancient activities in the village, and boats came along the river to collect the bark. Possibly because of movements along faults in the Woolhope Dome, several earth tremors have been recorded, most notable being on 17th December 1896, when several buildings were damaged.

Mordiford

The village originated at a ford, but a bridge has been there for a long time, and the main western arch is from 1352, though the bridge mostly dates from the 16th century. The Battle of Mordiford Bridge took place in the Civil War. Mordiford still has a mill, a spring called The Spout, and is famous for its Corn Dollies, made of straw but often with hops included. Mordiford is famous too for its dragon – it was pictured on the outside of Holy Rood church tower, but can no longer be seen. It was green, with a 12ft long body, and red mouth and tongue. Next to the Norman church is the former rectory, a Georgian brick house, with wonderful views across the river and old bridge. Milling was important in the past, and the mill on Pentaloe Brook has been restored. The River Lugg used to be important for navigation, and weirs went up as far as Leominster. Evidence of one of the old weirs can be seen beneath the bridge.

The Walk

Start from Fownhope church (1), and walk back to the main road through the village and turn left. Pass the Green Man and the New Inn (with its notice welcoming Ramblers) before reaching the cross roads. To the left is the old ferry and another pub, and across on the right is the old pump, a memorial for the diamond jubilee of Queen Victoria on 20th June 1897. Keep going along the road, to pass the village stores/post office, and at the end of the village, where a footpath comes in from the left, we go right over a stile with two footpaths. Once over the stile turn left along the hedge to walk parallel with the road, through two fairly large fields, to reach a stile in the corner of the second field. Go over this and down to the road, where we need to cross over to a narrow path, and turn left to retrace steps for about 100 metres along the road, to reach a footpath turning right.

Follow this track which soon bends left, and then leads out into a large open field, on the flood plain of the River Wye. Go straight ahead along the line of the track, and at the end of the field, turn right alongside a hedge, to reach a stile at the end of the hedge. Sparrowhawks and herons were amongst the interesting birds seen in this area. Go over the stile and straight across the middle of the next field (potatoes in 1999), and then over another stile and across the next, and much larger field, passing to the left of a small clump of trees, with a fragment of hedge to our left. Head towards a tall tree near the far right corner of this field and arrive at the river bank, where probably *Quiet flows the Wye*, unlike last winter when the river had a few rather angry periods.

Turn right alongside the Wye, to a stile, and then cross a small field to a kissing gate, and the beginning of the tents and caravans. This site is set in a quite idyllic location, with willows and other

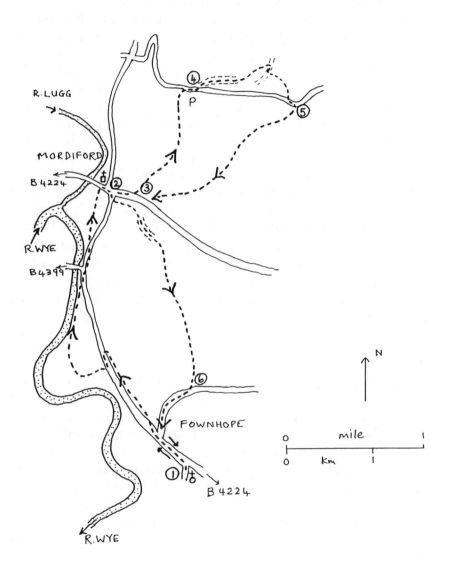

trees lining the river, and beautiful countryside all around, with the steep wooded slope of West Wood over to our right.

At the far end of the site is a shop, probably with swallows whizzing around; we proceed out to the road, and turn left. Beware of traffic. Before reaching the bridge (carrying the B4399 road to Holme Lacy, Rotherwas and Hereford) cross over to a small footpath on the other side of the road, which climbs slightly to pass through a wooded area rich in wild flowers and butterflies, before descending to the road again. Turn right and cross over, passing a house on the left, and soon reach a footpath going left, through a small patch of rough ground. This leads to two stiles, beyond which our path follows the hedge on our right through a large field. This prolific hedge is very popular with birds and we were accompanied by a redstart flicking its way along the hedge ahead of us. Go over a stile at the end of the field and keep straight ahead to the right of the farm buildings

Pass to the right of the farm buildings and over another stile on to a track. Keep straight ahead over the stream to reach the Village Post Office, where we turn right for the onward walk, but first turn left to have a look at the old bridge over the River Lugg, and to visit the church. The Village shop sells refreshments including home made cakes.

Short Cut

Walk through the village and for the **Short Cut** walk to Fownhope turn right at The Moon Inn **(2)**, following the sign towards Ross and Fownhope on the B4224. Cross the small stream and then go left across the road to follow the footpath sign for the Wye Valley Walk and a yellow arrow to lead us through the yard of Mill House to reach a metal gate. (The Old Mill is about 100 metres further along the main road). Keep straight ahead along the right margin of two small fields, to a stile, beyond which head diagonally right through an orchard, in which sheep may be grazing. At the end of this field reach a stile and go on to a path between hedges, which leads up to a few houses.

Turn left along the driveway, passing Bagpiper Cottage on the right. Keep ahead as far as the large farm complex, where we turn right along a stony track passing between farm buildings. Move out into open country, with West Woods covering the top of the hill over to the right. Pass a small isolated house on the left, where a path goes off to the right, and soon reach another house on the left, which commands excellent views across to the wooded hills of Fownhope Park, on the ridge of Silurian rocks. Buzzards are often to be seen and heard around here, as well as twittering swallows, finches and many other birds.

Reach a large gate, and keep straight ahead, with a hedge on the left, and woods on hill tops to right and left. On the Cambrian rocks to the left is Haugh Wood, one of the largest woodlands in Herefordshire and now managed by the Forestry Commission. Go over the stile at the end of the field and straight across the middle of the next field. The path comes alongside a few trees on the left, where I heard a loud hammering noise which turned out to be a Great Spotted Woodpecker trying to crack open a hazelnut. Follow the hedge through which the buildings of Nupend will soon be seen, as we begin to descend to a gate, a driveway, a small stream, and the Fownhope to Woolhope road **(6)**.

The sign of the trout and the Wye Valley Walk crosses the road and goes straight on, but we turn right to follow the country road down into Fownhope. The road is lined with varied hedgerows with fruits, berries and wild flowers. Up to the right are the woods on the side of Cherry Hill, which is topped by an old fort, as well as a variety of trees including some ancient yews, and cherry trees which are colourful with blossom in the spring.

At the cross roads, by the old memorial pump, turn left to return to our starting point, perhaps trying one of the excellent possibilities for refreshment in this village, regarded by many as the most picturesque in the County – quite a claim, as there is plenty of competition!

Main walk

For the Main Walk continue past the Moon Inn **(2)** on our left, and a telephone box on the right, and proceed on the pavement alongside the road to Haugh Wood and Woolhope. Just over 100 metres along the road, a signpost for Mordiford Loop Walk points left **(3)**, up a steep stony track and we follow this, with houses just to our right. As this track begins to bend right, at a Private Notice, go left along the footpath up a few steps and into the woods. Follow the path as it climbs fairly steeply at first, and as it begins to level off, reach the end of the wood. If you are the first to pass through the wood today, you may have to break through many spiders' webs across the path. Go over the stile and straight ahead into an open field, with a hedge on our right. Pheasants may be numerous around here, as we continue to climb slightly, admiring the views opening out to the left, from our elevated position on the ridge of Silurian limestone, part of the Woolhope Dome, a famous Geological feature where folded 500 million years old Cambrian rocks outcrop.

At the top of the slope, our path bends left, with a line of trees and small wood on our left. At the end of the field go through an iron gate (or over the stile alongside) and keep straight ahead across the next narrow field, at the end of which is Checkley Barn Picnic Place. We keep straight ahead through the gate, alongside which is a round cattle drinking trough, and like the more common elongated trough, this is accessible to animals in either of the two fields. As we cross this field, we can admire the views over the Lugg Valley to the left, with Hereford in the distance. Reach a stile, over which is a small wood, and a signpost. The Swardon Quarry Picnic Place and Viewpoint is 150 m to our left, if required, but our onward route is to the right (Checkley 1.5km), soon reaching a narrow road **(4)**.

Walk along the road for about 100 metres before going left on a stony track which ascends steadily. Almost immediately it divides and we keep left, straight ahead really. The track is on loose stones and also on exposures of the Silurian rock, almost like paving in places, as it climbs steadily between lines of trees which are really overgrown hedges.

As it levels off, we reach a junction of paths. Sharp left and back is a narrow path which leads to Priors Court, and passes close to the triangulation point on Backbury Hill, which is up to our left. Straight ahead, the track splits, with a narrow path forking left towards the hill fort on Backbury, but we take the right fork still following the bridleway sign and beginning to descend. Passing through mixed deciduous woodland with undergrowth, and rich in wildlife, we may find crab apples on the floor, as well as hazelnuts.

Ignore a narrow path going right and downhill, and just keep going, with sight and sound of a few houses down to our right. Our path bends left and continues to descend, between hedges rich in fruits including a few damsons and berries. At a broad stony track and T-junction, turn right following the Circular Walk sign, towards the house on our right. Opposite the house is a footpath where we turn left over the stile. Cross a field going downhill to a marker post by a large ash tree and hedges laden with hawthorn berries, elder berries and hips. Go steeply downhill for a few metres to another stile and cross the middle of the next field to the left of the lone oak tree. Go over the next stile and across the middle of the next field to the left of a lone telegraph post, to a stile and out on to the road (5).

Turn left along the road for about 200 metres and as the road bends left, we turn right at the signpost (and map) for the Mordiford Loop, along a track between hedges, with a black and white house to our left. Reach a stile by a gate and keep straight ahead across a narrow field with a few apple trees to our left. Go over another stile and cross the field beyond, to another stile and field. Up to our right is a good view of the wooded peak of Backbury Hill.

Just keep straight on over stiles and across fields, then cross a track, and two more fields, with the buildings of Warslaw up to our right. All the stiles on this stretch are slightly awkward as they are really fences, with no step to help walkers climb over. The small Pentaloe Brook, the source of energy for the Mordiford Mill, has been to our left all the time.

Cross a footbridge to enter the woods and then follow the clear path through Bear's Wood, still close to Pentaloe Brook. The wood is mixed deciduous, with some signs of former coppicing of the hazel.

Cross the stream over a wooden footbridge with stiles at both ends, and notice the fine outcrop of horizontally bedded sands and shales on the right, where the stream has carved a small gorge. The stream is now on our right.

Reach a clearing and a forestry track (Haugh Wood is up to our left), with a ford across the river, but we keep straight ahead. Through the trees across the river, an open field can be seen, as we reach an area of coniferous trees. As the track narrows to a path, look for a right turn, and we descend slightly towards an old ruin (in need of modernisation the Estate Agent might say) and go through a gate and out of the wood. Head down across the grass towards the gravel driveway and continue along this, with the open field on the left and trees on the right.

At the end of the field pass through a gateway, and as the driveway begins to bend left, go right towards the river, aiming to pass to the right side of the houses ahead. Once down by the stream, the grassy field is now on our left, with stream and trees to our right, and up to the left can be seen the wooded hill of West Wood beyond which is the caravan site alongside the Wye, seen earlier.

At the end of the field is a narrow path between houses and gardens, and then we reach a narrow road, where we turn right. As this road ends, keep ahead along another narrow path to emerge on to the main road, where we turn right. We soon pass the start of the Mordiford Loop **(3)**, and about 100 metres to the left at the far side of the field is a hedge along which we will walk for the continuation when we leave Mordiford. Reach the Moon Inn **(2)** and turn left along the road towards Fownhope for about 30 metres. Then, follow the instruction mentioned in the short cut above.

September
Monmouth to Redbrook

The valley downstream from Monmouth is steep sided and particularly beautiful with its wooded slopes. The steep climb to the Kymin gives views over Monmouth and into the Welsh Hills, whilst near Redbrook and Newland the views take in the hills and woods of the Forest of Dean.

Lengths of walks: The two separate walks are 8 miles (4 hours) and 6 miles (3 hours) respectively but can be linked together to give a longer 12-mile walk.

Terrain: flat near the river, but undulating elsewhere, with a steep climb up to the Kymin and from Lower Redbrook. Parts of the walk may be muddy.

Map: O.S. Outdoor Leisure 14, Wye Valley and Forest of Dean, or Landranger 162.

Starting point: for the Monmouth walk, GR506125, and in Redbrook, GR536099. Monmouth is at the crossing point of the A40 and A466, and Redbrook is on the A466 Monmouth to Chepstow road.

Public Transport: a bus service runs along the A466.

Facilities: Monmouth has car parks, a wide choice of pubs and cafés, a bus station and a Tourist Information Centre (01600 713899). There is a pub in Lower Redbrook and another in Newland.

Weather

Noted for its mixture of summery and autumnal weather, the month lived up to this reputation in 1999, with a good anticyclonic spell early in the month, followed by some wet and windy low pressure weather. Hot and sunny weather was experienced for nearly two weeks, though the lower angle of the sun and the shorter days than those of July and August meant that dews occurred and could be clearly seen on the grass and on spiders' webs. The highest September temperatures for 50 years were recorded during this spell (up to 29°C on the 4th and 5th), and these contributed to the entire month being warmer than average. Rain arrived on the 16th, coinciding with the end of the cricket season, and continued until the end of the month. A few days suffered from continuous rain, but generally the rainfall came in showers – some of which were very heavy. A few days were reminiscent of April showery days, but the showers were much heavier, as a result of the effects of summer heating of the land. A few of the showers gave thunder and lightning, large hailstones fell in several storms, and small tornadoes and waterspouts were seen. By the end of the month, temperatures were cooling down to the seasonal average, having generally been above the norm. Is this a result of global warming, or merely variations within the range we always experience? In addition to the warmer than average temperatures, the rainfall figures were also well above average, with river levels reaching near the top of their banks.

The Countryside

The countryside remained very green throughout this wet month, and gradually the colour of wild flowers faded. In the hedges, old man's beard spread rapidly, though still green in colour, and bindweed was rampant, with white flowers becoming abundant. Red hips, black elderberries and blackberries also provided variations from the general green theme. In the fields of the Wye valley greenery also dominated with sheep and cattle grazing quietly on the lush pastures, but one field of sunflowers and a few fields of maize still contain their crops. The few cereal fields have been harvested, and some have already been ploughed up, showing the brownish-red soils of Herefordshire, distinctive in colour because of the local sandstones, though not as red as the soils of Devon. A few butterflies are to be seen on sunny days, and birds are ever-present, though small birds are still not easily seen in the leafy trees. Towards the end of the month, the first leaves had turned to yellow, brown or even red. Shelley, in his 'Ode to the West Wind' wrote:

> *O wild west wind, though breath of Autumn's being*
> *Thou, from whose unseen presence the leaves dead*
> *Are driven, like ghosts from an enchanter fleeing*
> *Yellow and black and pale and hectic red.*

Summer visitors are still present, notably a few warblers, but most numerous are the house martins often gathering in large numbers now, preparing themselves for the long migration Also in large numbers are starlings, and rooks and jackdaws too are seen in flocks. Even crows are in groups nowadays. A few finches are beginning to

Tawny owl

flock although perhaps many are just overgrown families, but the most interesting gangs of birds are those of the tits. These seem to gather several varieties of birds together as they work their way round woodland from tree to tree, as though on a circuit looking for food, which is abundant at this time of year. The gangs of small birds, constantly twittering or sissing are mainly blue tits, but will often be accompanied by a few great tits, coal tits and long tailed tits, as well as one or two warblers, a group of goldcrests and perhaps a tree creeper as well. The **bird of the month** is the tawny owl, also known as the brown owl, and in woodland areas can be heard calling. This is a time of year when they get noisy, as they try to establish territories for the winter. In a poem of 1616, Thomas Vanter wrote:

> *Thou singest alone sitting by night,*
> *Te whit, te whoo, te wit, te wit.*

Rarely seen during the day unless noticed when a snoozing owl is being mobbed by small birds, the owl mainly feeds on mice and voles but occasionally catches small birds and will eat worms. Its shrill call of *kewick* is often heard during the night.

Monmouth

The history of this ancient town includes periods of Roman and Norman control, and remains of the Norman castle can still be seen today, on the banks of the Monnow. Henry V was born in this castle in 1387, and he is remembered by the statue on the Shire Hall, which is located in Agincourt Square. The Shire Hall dates from 1724 and is on the site of an Elizabethan market. It now contains the Tourist Information Centre and in the small market place is a statue to Mr.

Statues of Henry V and Charles Rolls at the Shire Hall

Rolls (of Rolls Royce fame), who lived nearby in Hendre. Lady Llangattock, the mother of Charles Rolls collected relics of Lord Nelson, which are now in the Nelson Museum, together with exhibitions depicting the history of the town. Amongst other features of interest in Monmouth are the Castle and Regimental Museum, the churches, schools, the old gaol and the 13th-century stone gated bridge over the River Monnow (unique in Britain and one of only three in Europe) The Free Grammar School was founded in 1615 by William Jones, and has been run by the Haberdashers' Company, as has the Girls' School.

Redbrook

The village grew as an industrial centre in the 1690s when workers from Sweden established a copper works, where the football pitch is now situated. About 100 years later a tinplate works was established here, and this did not finally close until 1961. Industrial growth was helped by the construction of a railway in 1812, linking Redbrook to the iron and coal mines in the Forest of Dean. Trucks were lowered down the steep slope at Redbrook on an inclined plane. Lower Redbrook now has a school and the small church of St Saviour, which dates from 1873. Penallt, across the river from Redbrook, was famous for its pudding stone (or breccia) millstones, some of which are visible in the river. Also across the river is the Boat Inn, at the site of an ancient ferry, but now reached by the footbridge alongside the old railway bridge. This Wye Valley Railway line was opened in 1876, but closed in 1959.

The Kymin

Owned by the National Trust since 1902, when it was given by the people of Monmouthshire, this round house and the surrounding 3.8 ha. (nearly 10 acres) is situated on the top of the valley wall, where the sandstone is capped with some quartz conglomerate. Stunning views over the town look towards the Brecon Beacons and lines of Welsh hills. Built in 1793, as a summerhouse, it was used as a banqueting house by the local gentry in the past, but is now a private residence. Close by is the Naval Temple, opened in 1801 to commemorate naval triumphs, and to serve as a monument to several Admirals, including Lord Nelson, who visited here in 1802.

The Kymin

Newland

This village first built its church in the 13th century, and nowadays the famous All Saints church is often called the 'Cathedral of the Forest'. It is most noted for its impressive tower, with pinnacles and parapet. Inside the church are very broad aisles, a decorated font from the 17th century, several stained glass windows and several ancient effigies, one of which is probably 13th century and is Robert De Wakering, the founder of the church. Notice the lack of pews in this church, as for most of its life the large nave and aisles had no seats, because it was used as a community centre for the area. The religious part of the church only began at the chancel steps. The churchyard is bordered by 17th- and 18th-century houses, which surround the large grassy close. On the south side are Alms Houses dating from 1615 and founded by William Jones (founder of the school in Monmouth). Although born in Newland, it was in London that Jones made his fortune as a Haberdasher. To the west of the churchyard is the former Bell Grammar School, with an inscription to Edward Bell, 1639.

The Monmouth – Kymin – Redbrook Walk

This is an 8-mile walk but can be linked to the Redbrook circuit to give a longer 12-mile walk if required. We begin in Agincourt Square **(1)** and walk along Church Street. Turn right at the parish church of St Mary, which has Norman foundations but was mostly rebuilt in 1880. Pass the sandstone Roman Catholic church which dates from 1792, and just before the T-junction note the buildings of Monmouth School on right and left, and on the wall opposite is lettering to say this was a Grammar School and is now a Haberdashers' School. Turn left here and then right towards the main road, A40, which we underpass to reach an information board about the Wye Valley Walk and then the bridge over the River Wye. Note the Monmouth School Sports Centre on the left, and their playing fields on the right. The road soon splits, right being the A466 to Tintern but we go left along the A4136 towards the Forest of Dean. Shortly after this road bends left near the May Hill hotel, look for a path on the right, signposted Kymin Road, Offa's Dyke Path, and Wysis Way. The path leads up into the woods, which are still very green though with a few fallen leaves on the floor. Many ferns, including some lovely hart's tongue, grow near to our path.

Emerge from the woods to a small kissing gate, cross the edge of a field to another gate and out on to a driveway where we turn left. This leads to a narrow road and we keep straight ahead here, climbing, between lush hedges, with masses of the still greenish old man's beard climbing over everything. Where the road bends right **(2)** and there is a Water Reservoir (Dwr Cymru – Welsh Water) on the left, we go straight ahead over the stile by a gate, for a steep climb through Garth Woods. We are still following Offa's Dyke Path, which we shall continue to do so as far as the road leading into Upper Redbrook.

At the top of this wood, there is a notice concerning Fiddler's

Elbow National Nature Reserve, where mature oak and beech woods contain a wide range of plants and animals. Felling and coppicing is carried out to keep a balance of light and shade, and young and older trees. Young trees are fenced round as a protection from the deer. Go right, over a stile and up through an open field, towards a house and a mast, and to a stile at the top corner. Turn left along the driveway for 20 metres and then go left, through a gate into more woods, and another steep climb. These woods are gloomy with conifers at first, but as we climb up through a sunken path with exposed tree roots,

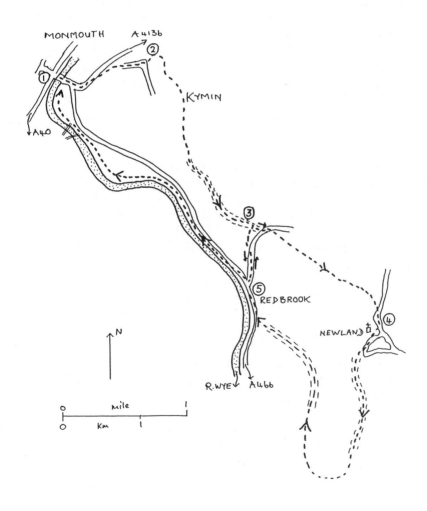

note the white pebbles of quartz in the rocks. Many of these have been weathered out and are loose on the path, evidence of the way that rocks are weathered and broken up.

Emerge from the top of this wood, at the level of the Kymin, which is just a few metres over to the right. The views make the climb worth while, with a useful map to name a few of the peaks to be seen, notably Sugar Loaf in the Brecon Beacons, and the steep slope of Hay Bluff. The viewpoint is at 250 metres (820ft). A few metres along from the house is the Temple, with names of admirals, and Britannia sitting proudly and impressively on top.

Walk on through the trees to reach a car parking area, and where the narrow road leads off to the right, go straight ahead through an iron kissing gate along a path between fences. After reaching another kissing gate the path continues along the margin of fields, with good views to the left and the woods on our right. At the end of the first field, go over a stile and along a narrow path between wire fence and trees, and then over another stile to cross a field, to another stile and then the third field. Up to the left, on top of the hill, are the buildings of Upper Beaulieu farm. Reach the end of the woods and go over a stile by a converted barn, on to a track where we turn left and gradually descend. Follow this track, Duffield's Lane, for more than half a mile and shortly beyond the large farm complex to the left (Duffield's Farm) the track splits **(3)**.

For the **Longer Walk**, take the left fork here if wishing to extend the walk to 12 miles by going via Newland, as described later in the Redbrook walk.

The major route at this fork goes right as the Offa's Dyke Path, which we follow to pass Hafan, and descend fairly steadily to join the B road on its way through Upper Redbrook. Continue down this road, passing beneath the bridge (route of the old trackway) and along the pavement to descend to the Wye Valley and, at the main road, the A466 **(5)**, we turn right. Lower Redbrook is mainly to the left, and the Boat Inn is there if required, but for Monmouth, we cross over the main road and turn right along the footpath. This is the route of the Wye Valley Walk. After a few hundred metres, the pavement ends and we go left to follow the footpath alongside the river. At first, there is just a narrow field between the river and the road, then a small wood, beyond which the fields open out, but we stay close to the river bank.

We just follow the riverside path, very close to the road for about a mile, and then after passing through a few trees, the river bends away from the road, but we stay close to the river bank, as we move into an open field. This field on our right widens out.

In the river are a few rocks, and then several of the rock and concrete fingers extending into the river, to increase the flow of the water as an encouragement to the fish. The banks here are lined with masses of undergrowth, grasses and wild flowers, including the tall rose bay willow herb, and the even taller Indian or Himalayan balsam which has spread so widely along the Wye. Its seeds pop out with a small explosion and, as some shoot into the river, they are washed downstream and can easily colonise along all the banks. Many flowers are past their best by September, but the riverside still looks very lush. Trees, notably willow, line the bank. Across on the other bank are a couple of open meadows and then the Livox Woods come down to clothe the bank, for the next half-mile or so.

The path continues along the margin of the fields, passing several former stiles, but no longer necessary as all the fields have been merged into one. Relics of former hedges stretching out to our right can be seen in places, and up to the right is the road, beyond which is the wooded hillside. This large field in 2000 was growing maize, a very rich and successful crop it appeared to be too.

Birds that may be seen along here include heron, cormorant, ducks, and swans (with nearly fully-grown cygnets). Early in the month there may be swallows, house martins and sand martins flying low over the water (some of the sand martins having bred near to the Monnow Bridge), with warblers, tits and finches in the dense vegetation.

Monnow Bridge

After nearly a mile in this large field, we reach a wire fence and a building which is the Sewage Works, but continue along the river side, passing the old railway viaduct and then an iron railway bridge, before reaching the playing fields of Monmouth School. Walk on around the edge of these to the Pavilion and then the main road where we turn left, and make use of the underpass to walk into the town.

The Redbrook to Newland Walk

This is a 6-mile circuit, beginning with a steep climb, but then becomes more gentle walking. From Redbrook downstream to Tintern the Wye flows in a gorge cut into the Lower Devonian rocks of the Forest of Dean plateau. The river has been rejuvenated, which is why it cut its gorge, but as a result of this rejuvenation it abandoned a large meander which contains Newland, about 110 metres (370ft) above the present river level at Redbrook.

Car parking is available between the road and the river **(5)**, at each end of the football pitch. The more southerly is the car park for the Boat Inn, reached by the footbridge across the river, adjacent to the old railway bridge. This pub is situated close to the Offa's Dyke Path as well as being on the Wye Valley Walk, so is very popular with walkers.

From the car park walk along the main road A466 towards Monmouth passing the school on the right, and St Saviour's Chapel. Turn right on the B4231 at the Osteopathic Centre, formerly a pub, The Bush Inn, following the signpost to Newland, Clearwell and Coleford. The first house on the right is the Old Brewery, with an old water wheel, and the noise of a fast flowing stream can be heard as we climb steadily. Remnants of old copper workings can be seen to our right, just before we reach the bridge crossing over the road. This formerly carried an industrial tramway.

Beyond the bridge there is no pavement, as we climb steadily between the houses of Upper Redbrook, passing Mill Cottage and then the Old Inn (Queen's Head). As the road bends slightly to the right, look for the surfaced track on the left, which is followed by Offa's Dyke Path, signed 3 miles to Monmouth: this is our route for a few hundred metres. Pass behind houses with their gardens terraced to cope with the steepness of the slope in this narrow valley, holding a tributary to the Wye. Keep left when the track divides, and soon pass the house named Hafan. About 30 metres beyond here the track divides but the main route goes to the left (to the Kymin and Monmouth – the route of the main walk from Monmouth), and here is where we turn sharp right.

It is at this point that we meet the walk from Monmouth (3). Having turned sharp right, we descend on a trackway overgrown by trees, including several chestnuts, and pass behind the back of a house. The track is floored by rocks and has been gullied by the effects of running water. Look for the evidence of an old railway line to the left, as we descend to the road, where we reach a signpost pointing back to Wyesham and Kymin.

Cross the road and turn right for 10 metres to reach a path pointing left, leading down to a footbridge over a small stream, which is feeding the large Mill Pool just visible to the right. Climb steeply up the other side of this narrow valley through the trees to reach a stile, and go on across the middle of the open field. Good views open up to the left and back up towards Duffield's Farm (and Upper Beaulieu Farm beyond). Come alongside the edge of a wood on our right and follow this to near the corner of the field, where we reach a stile and a path leading us on through the woods (called Furnace Grove – further evidence of former industrial uses in this area). Continue climbing through the wood, with its bright green harts' tongue and other ferns, to reach a stile at the top.

Go on over the stile and diagonally left towards the edge of the wood and the corner of this field. Keep ahead over the gate and along the right margin of the field, but just before the end of this field go right, over a stile and turn immediately left to walk along the edge of the field, to another stile in the corner. Beyond the stile pass through a small wood, over a wet patch, to a stile and another field, with a line of trees on our left, and a wood across at the other side of the field.

At the end of this field is a stile and about 50 metres beyond this go left over another stile but turn right to walk alongside the hedge. As this leads downhill, the church tower and other buildings of Newland come into sight. Go through the gate and keep straight ahead alongside the hedge for 30 metres and then head diagonally right over to the far corner of the field and a stile and out on to the narrow road into Newland, opposite the Old Forge and near the Village Room. Turn right here to pass a large farm and other large stone buildings, to reach the 13th-century Ostrich Inn on the left and the imposing All Saints Church on the right **(4)**.

Our onward route takes us diagonally across the churchyard, with Alms Houses to the left, and the former Bell Grammar School on the right, to reach the road again, where we descend steeply down Savage Hill to a T-junction at the bottom, where we turn right. After a few metres turn left just before the stables, along the narrow road signed 'Road used as a public path', to walk away from the village, passing the large Sewage Works on our left. We follow the surfaced road, which becomes a gravel track, as the walk continues near the bottom of the large valley. This is an old route of the River Wye, which was abandoned when the river had renewed powers of erosion and cut down to its present level. We follow this valley as it curves in a meander, bending to the right, following the track leading to Lodges Farm. Just before reaching these buildings, we pass an old building on the left, then a small pond on the left. Before reaching the buildings of Lodges Farm, we are pointed to the right, through a metal gate, to pass 20-30 metres to the side of the farm, now following a grassy track, with a pond on our right, where the small stream has been dammed. This stream is Valley Brook, which follows the course of the old Wye meander for the two miles round to Redbrook. As we follow the grassy track, the stream is to our right. We reach an iron gate with a yellow arrow pointing us straight ahead, and we walk on through a beautiful open valley with grassy slopes on either side, though with woodland at the top of both valley sides. As this track continues, fairly level, it bends round to the right, staying fairly close to the stream.

The isolated house we soon reach, is Birts Cottage, and we pass it via the stile to the right, and join on to their driveway, which is a grassy track with gravel strips to provide dry and firm ground for the wheels of vehicles. We cross the stream at an old stone bridge and then get into a fenced driveway, along which there are several gates.

As we pass Birts Cottage, up to the right is Astridge Wood and up to the left is Highbury plains, and both of these hills have a thin cap of Lower Carboniferous limestone. The core of the meander, which is to our right at this time, is a fragment of the Forest of Dean plateau.

As we head northwards towards Redbrook, along the fenced track, we pass through a series of gates, pass a pond on our left, where ducks and a pair of barnacle geese were seen on our last visit. Wild flowers are abundant around here, and a few unusual trees have been planted. Continuing along the track we reach another small pond, and pass a path going off to the right, just before the point where the track splits. We take the right fork, which leads us along the right side of the river, with good views across to Glyn Farm and adjacent buildings, with terraced gardens.

Our track soon joins the driveway leading to Glyn Farm and Glyn Barn and at this point there is a very good view back to look at the curve of the old meander we have been following for a couple of miles. Our fairly level track crosses over the stream, again, now it has moved to our right, as we pass an isolated house and then soon see the first buildings of Redbrook. As we pass between the houses, views of the old railway bridge and the river and the football pitch come into view, and when we reach the concrete steps going down to our right, turn here, along the Offa's Dyke Path and descend to the bottom where a left turn leads to the main road. Turn right here to walk along to the starting point **(5)**, or walk on through the village and continue along the Monmouth road, if walking back into Monmouth.

October
Ross-on-Wye

Ross is a fascinating historic town set in beautiful countryside, and each of the two circular walks from Ross crosses farmland and ascends one of the steep hills overlooking the town. These two wooded hills, Penyard and Chase, are outliers of the Forest of Dean, and were formerly in the middle of a huge meander of the Wye, nearly 60 metres (200ft) above sea level, which was abandoned by the river when it changed its course thousands of years ago, and cut down to its present height of 30 metres (110ft). The two walks can be linked together if a longer walk is required.

Lengths of walks: the Rudhall and Penyard walk is 8 miles (3-4 hours) and the Chase Hill walk is nearly 6 miles. Linking the two together would give a walk of about 11 miles (5 hours).

Terrain: mostly flat but there is a steep climb and descent on each walk. Places are likely to be muddy and there are a few stiles to cross.

Map: O.S. Outdoor Leisure 14, Wye Valley and Forest of Dean; or Landranger 162.

Starting point: the Heritage Centre GR599242

Facilities: Ross can be reached along the M50, A40 or the A449, and has several car parks. It is accessible by bus, contains a Tourist Information Centre (01989 562768) and a wide choice of refreshments.

Weather

As usual the month experienced a wide range of weather, with periods of gales as well as calm spells, but it was a sunny month this year, and one of the sunniest this century, though not quite as sunny as 1959. About 120 hours of sunshine were recorded in most of England and Wales, which is about 25% above the average figure for this month. Temperatures were about average and the rainfall was generally slightly below average in spite of spells with heavy thundery showers early in the month and more heavy rainfall around the 10th of the month and during the last three days when low pressure brought a wet and windy end to the month. High pressure dominated around the 12th and again for a few days around the 25th. St Simon and St Jude's day (28th) is reputed to be *wet and windy*, but not this year as the weather was in a settled spell. Another of the saint's days St Luke (18th), is often thought to experience a dry spell, known as *St Luke's Little summer*, comparable to the more famous and longer lasting *Indian summer*. A short spell of high pressure was prevailing on St Luke's day but it did not last long, and brought cool temperatures with day maxima of only about 8°C, in contrast to many days in the month when maxima were up to 15°C (compared with an expected average of about 10-12°C).

The Countryside

Everywhere still looked very green at the beginning of the month, with generally mild and often warm weather. There were sufficient rainy days for the leaves to stay on the trees, and only in the final few days of the month were masses of leaves to be seen falling. Amongst the earliest of trees to be losing leaves is the sweet chestnut, which is also early to be showing gorgeous autumn colours. There is no need to go to New England to see the wonderful colours, just visit the Wye Valley. Many trees were prolific with fruits, including acorns, conkers and sweet chestnuts. Sunshine ripened good crops of alder, birch and conifer seeds. Red berries on the rowan, holly, hawthorn and hips were also providing rich sources of food for birds and animals. A few farm fields were showing the green of winter crops but a few were brown from recent ploughing, and many tractors were still at work in the fields – generally accompanied by opportunist birds notably the noisy gulls. Much of the Wye valley is in grass of course, and some grazing is still quite good, with fields of grazing sheep and cattle, in spite of the very hard times experienced by pastoral farmers recently. After a quiet spell for birds, a few were beginning to sing, especially late in the month, possibly after moulting. The robin is one of the first and most frequent, and on a sunny day even the skylark may be trying out its voice again. Birds are also noisy in their search for food amongst the dead leaves which cover the ground, even a blackbird making as much noise as the crunching boots of a walker, as it tosses leaves around in the search for juicy worms or insects. The noisiest in the leaves must be the strutting pheasants, the **bird of the month**. These non-migratory birds are not real natives, but were introduced to Europe generally, in pre Norman times, from the Caspian-Caucasus area and further east. The male is

Pheasant

very bright and colourful whilst the female is duller, with a shorter tail. Pheasant numbers are maintained by breeding, for subsequent release for shooting. More than 20 million are shot in a season, and as the land is managed for pheasants in what is a rural industry, pheasant rearing has a considerable, and beneficial, effect on countryside, preserving and maintaining woods and hedges. Pheasant often run and seem reluctant to fly, but eventually will take off explosively, especially the males, who are also very noisy with their abrupt and raucous calling. They can make you jump if you are walking nearby, making as much noise as large animals might do.

Other noisy birds, beside the pheasants, can be seen in the growing flocks of starlings, rooks, jackdaws and gulls searching for food in the fields. Early in the month there were the house martins too, but they disappeared at the time of a northerly spell about the 10th of the month. They were soon replaced by flocks of fieldfares, winter visitors, first seen around the 20th when easterly winds were blowing. The orchards in the fields around Ross were heavy with fruit this year, and fallen apples were appreciated by the wild life. Apple Day was celebrated in several localities in this area.

Ross-on-Wye

Ross is perched on the cliff of a meander scar of the reddish sandstone of the Brownstone Series, part of the Lower Devonian geological period of 400 million years ago, when desert conditions prevailed. Ross was already a village at the time of Domesday, and it became a market centre in the 12th century when King Stephen granted a charter. The cattle market remains, slightly out of town

Ross-on-Wye and its parish church

near the main roads. Development as a tourist centre began in the 1770s when Ross was included in the Wye Tour, and tourism is still important to the local economy. The very informative Heritage Centre in the old red sandstone Market House is a good starting point for a visit to the town and is also the starting point of our walks. Opposite the Market House is the black and white house where John Kyrle lived. Nearby is the parish church of St Mary the Virgin which dates from the 13th century, and is a famous landmark with the 14th century spire rising to a height of 62m (205ft). Major renovation work took place in 1984. The church contains a monument to John Kyrle and many tablets and tombs to the Rudhall family, as well as several hedgehogs, the animal used as a symbol of the town. In the churchyard near the south-east corner of the church is the Plague Cross. From the hill top on which the church stands are magnificent views across the Wye plain, especially from the Prospect. Also on the hill are the Royal Hotel and the 1833 Mock Gothic Town Walls with the Gazebo Tower, which was repaired in 1997.

John Kyrle

Described as the 'Man of Ross' by the poet Alexander Pope, John Kyrle (1637-1724) was born in Dymock but spent most of his life in Ross. He became a great benefactor to the town, providing a water supply, repairing the church spire in 1721, and laying out the Prospect Gardens in 1696. The John Kyrle Walk is a three-mile circuit, taking in many outstanding features of the town as well as the Wye riverside, across meadows of the Cleeve Estate which were owned by John Kyrle.

John Kyrle House

Weston-under-Penyard

The parish church of St Lawrence dates from the 12th century when it was within the parish of Ross-on-Wye, not becoming a parish church until 1683. Built of the local sandstone, with ashlar dressing, there have been many alterations over the centuries, with a major restoration in 1867. The nave still has its Norman arches, and the fine timbered porch and the tower both date from the 14th century.

The Rudhall and Penyard Walk

Set off from the Market Hall (1) in the centre of Ross-on-Wye, following the signpost to the Library, Bus Station and Antique Centre, along a one way street for traffic. Fork left just past the old church, which is the Antique Centre and walk along Cantilupe Road past the Library, and down to the major road. Cross over to the footpath and surfaced driveway along the right side of Safeways. This leads through an industrial estate to a caravan site, and we go through a small kissing gate by a large metal gate, and after a few metres go right to another kissing gate and into a field. Follow the left margin of this field, passing a small lake on the right, with coots and perhaps a cormorant. The caravan site is to our left.

At the end of the field go over a stile and up a few steps then cross the A40 (quickly), and down a few steps, and the footpath bends left, then over a stile and along the left margin of the field. The small stream is to our left as we continue over a stile and along the field margin, passing a footbridge but going on to the stile at the end of the field and on again to the end of the next field. Go over another stile, and pass to the left of a small pond, and bend slightly left to cross the stream over a farm bridge, and through an iron gate. Continue along the left margin of the next field, over a footbridge and straight across to the fence and hedge where we turn right along a grassy track. Up to our left can be seen the traffic on the M50.

At the end of the field, go through a metal gate and along a track between a wall and hedge. Reach a narrow road (2) and turn right to walk past the impressive gateway to Rudhall House, and admire the gardens and pools. At the T-junction, turn right towards Bromsash and Weston-under-Penyard, passing Rudhall Mill and Rudhall Barns, built of the local sandstone, which gives a warm glow, if the sun is shining. There may be sand on the road in places, washed out of adjacent fields.

Follow the lane between hedges, as it winds through glorious countryside, with May Hill to be seen over to the left. Pass through the hamlet of Kingstone and then, just before reaching the next houses on the left, there is a stile on the right. We go over here and walk along the left margin of the field for about 130 metres and then go left over a stile into the orchard. Turn right alongside the hedge, and at the end of the orchard, go left along the line of windbreak trees and then straight on across an open field, following the line of tele-graph poles. Penyard Hill is ahead, and away to our right is Ross-on-Wye. Reach a short driveway by a stone house, and at the road turn right to walk down towards Weston-under-Penyard, with some impressive old buildings. At the main road is the Weston Cross Inn, and we go nearly straight ahead on to the narrow road going steeply up to the church of St Lawrence (3).

Just above the church, the track divides and we fork right along a hedged lane, following a public footpath sign. When we reach the edge of the Penyard Woods, the track divides again and we fork right along a clear, broad and gravelled track, climbing steadily. At the

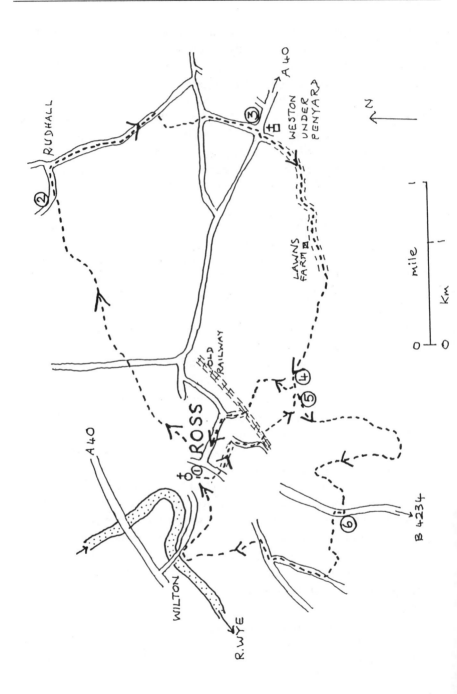

next junction bend sharp left, and steeply up, along the main track. At a junction of tracks, turn right to level off, with an open field to the left and woods to the right. Reach a gate and keep straight ahead with open fields on both sides, and good views over the Forest to the left. Pass Lawns Farm (height 173m, 567ft) and large barns, and keep ahead along a grassy track to a gate and then along the right margin of a field. Pheasants, cattle and various breeds of sheep are likely to be seen around here.

As the edge of the field approaches the woods on the right, there is a stile on the right. Down to the left across the field can be seen the last remnants of the old Penyard Castle, some stones from which were used in the buildings of Lawns Farm. Go over the stile and follow the path along the margin of the woods, with the open fields to the right. The path climbs slightly at first, and is floored with leaves and, in places, large numbers of sweet chestnuts, which make this a very crunchy stretch of walking. As we begin to descend slightly the path goes into the woods for a while and then emerges alongside a small field again, before heading more decisively into the woods, where beech trees are numerous. Reach a broad track where we turn right, and descend slightly. As it levels off, and then begins to bend to the right, we go left down to a stile and along the left margin of a small field, descending quite steeply, with a lovely valley to our left and wonderful views of the Welsh hills straight ahead.

Near the bottom of the field, as the fence bends left, like a dog leg, we go right **(4)**, by an oak tree and a small wooden marker post, to join the Wye Valley Walk and a Public Footpath. If intending to take the LONGER route (a further 5 miles), turn left here, along the field margin to reach a stile and a stone seat **(5)**, then follow the instructions given in the Chase Wood walk.

For the continuation of the Penyard Walk (a further 2 miles), go right here along a narrow path going downhill, and the path soon broadens into a track, and leads down to a gate and stile, and a further 20 metres to another stile. (Just beyond this is a wired off building – a small reservoir) Once over this stile turn left, and go steeply down to the bottom left corner of the field, on to a well worn path, where we turn left.

Pass through an old iron kissing gate and follow the Wye Valley Walk through trees, to reach a driveway alongside Alton Court. Just keep straight ahead on to a larger road, Penyard Lane. Turn left at the major road, and then take the second on the right alongside a large stone wall, to lead us through towards the centre of Ross.

Chase Wood Walk

From the Market Hall (1) walk along High Street towards the TIC and then turn left to pass the church. From the church, head south across the churchyard, leaving via an iron gate, a Memorial to James Wallace Richard Hall, Solicitor, Banker, Benefactor 1799-1860, who donated these gates. Turn right across the small car park, and walk on the path between the bowling green on the left and putting course on the right. Just before reaching the road, pass the Ross Weather Station on the left. At the road, the 'Prince of Wales' pub is on the right, but we go left across the road to reach a narrow footpath between walls and gardens, following the Wye Valley Walk sign. Cross the end of a small road, but keep straight ahead along the footpath to reach a road where we turn right. The Wye Valley Way soon turns left, but we continue straight along the road, which begins to bend left. After this bend, the road turns right, but we bear left along Lakeside Drive, to reach the end of the houses.

Pass through a gate, cross the cycle track, the route of the old railway (Hereford to Gloucester, opened in 1855, and closed in 1964) and on through a wooden kissing gate. Proceed along the left side of a large field (noting Alton Court across the field on our left), climbing steadily up to the woods. Go through the gate, take the middle of the three paths into Merrivale Woods, and climb steadily up the steep slope. The sunken path passes through dense undergrowth overshadowed by a mixture of deciduous trees, shedding their leaves at this time of year. At the top of the slope is a stone seat (5) memorial to David Ursell (1931-1994) and a stile. Beyond the stile about 100 metres to the left is point (4), where the main walk descends from Penyard Park and Woods. This is a short cut route back to Ross if required, and alternatively, anyone walking the Penyard route looking for extra mileage, could join our route at this stone seat.

From the stone seat, follow the Wye Valley Walk along the permissive path in the top of the woods. This clear path leads close to the back of the buildings of Hill Farm, and through a gate on to an open patch where tracks meet. Keep straight ahead and as the track splits ignore the right fork that is going downhill, and fork left along the broad stony track still climbing slightly. When the track divides again after about 100 metres, take the left fork, and stay on this stony track as it continues to climb. Good views open down to the left, especially when the leaves have gone off the trees. Ignore the locked gate going right, and soon to the right can be seen part of the open fields which cover the top of the hill. The summit has a triangulation point at 203m (666ft), and is surrounded by an Iron Age hill-fort, used over 2000 years ago, but with no public right of way nowadays.

Our track is fairly level now, and heading in a southerly direction, to a point where the track divides, with the Wye Valley Walk going straight ahead as a narrow path. But we fork right here along the now-grassy track between grass and nettles, with mainly coniferous trees along this stretch. (bearing about 260 degrees). Pass a couple of magnificent redwood trees a few metres to the left of the path, and soon reach a split in the path, almost a T-junction.

Turn right here on a narrower and less frequented path. The undergrowth spreads on to the path as we head in a northerly direction, with many grasses and flowers including thistles and burdock, but brambles and nettles too. On reaching a few redwood trees the path splits, with the clearer path going right, almost in an easterly direction, but we follow the other route still heading north. Just before reaching an old fence, when clearer open ground of the hill top can be seen through the trees to our right, we turn left to head steeply downhill. Pass a few large rocks as we descend, still in a northerly direction. At a main track, we turn right for 20 metres and then left again, still descending steeply in woodland. The narrow path leads us downhill and near the bottom, as an open field becomes visible, it divides into several paths because of local use. Bear slightly right and continue in the woods, with the field on our left, to reach an area of larch trees and then walk near the margin of the woods, with the open field just beyond the hedge, and finally descending to a path and a gap where we can move left into the large open field. Turn right here to follow the hedge towards the row of houses at the bottom end of the field, then go left to walk alongside this row of houses. Good views to the left look back at the wooded

Chase Hill. Beyond the houses, at the end of the field turn right along the track to follow the field margin to a stile and on to the road, B4234 **(6)**.

Turn right along this road, and just before the old farm buildings and the 30 speed limit signs for Ross, and the Vine Tree, cross over to turn left. Follow the footpath sign, heading west along the field margin, in an area where blackcurrants are grown. Note the good views towards Symonds Yat away to our left. Cross the route of an old railway line and proceed along the margin of a second field, then turn left still following a hedge, and at the end of the field turn right to walk towards the cottages, where our footpath goes through the left side of a garden to reach a narrow road.

Turn right along the road and soon come into an area of houses, the Archenfield area of Ross. Turn left at a T-junction, and after a further 50 metres turn right at the next T-junction. Follow this road to where a footpath goes right, but we turn left along the narrow road (Cleeve Lane). At the last house keep ahead along the track, which becomes sunken and descends to the river plain, passing between steps which are along the route of the John Kyrle Circular Walk. Continue down the slope, with rocky outcrops to the right, and walk across an area of rough ground, wonderful for wild life, to reach the banks of the River Wye. Turn right to reach the old Wilton Bridge, built in 1597, with its rather worn 18th-century sun dial, with a gloomy verse, though offering sound advice: *'Esteem thy precious time which passes so swift away'* .

From the bridge, walk towards Ross, on the roadside or on the grass to the right, enjoying the sight of the graceful church spire. Pass an old iron pump and then reach the large car park, with playing fields to our right. At the far end of the car park is a map of the Wye Valley Walk, and an arrow pointing to the path climbing steeply through the woods. At the top of the slope reach a junction of paths where we turn right for a few metres following the John Kyrle Walk and Wye Valley Way sign, then go left through an iron kissing gate and on the footpath between fences. Reach a driveway where the Wye Valley Way goes right, but we keep straight ahead along another footpath, still on the John Kyrle Walk. At the next kissing gate we reach the churchyard, and retrace steps to our starting point.

November

Rhayader and Elan

The lush green valleys are surrounded by hills in all directions, and our walks gain enough height to see more hills stretching away in the distance. Man has added forests and lakes to this hilly environment and our walks visit examples of all these varied landscapes.

Lengths of walks: Rhayader, 6 miles – or only 4 if not going to Gigrin Farm. The Elan walk is about 4 miles, with the addition of Cnwch Wood circuit if required. It is easy to link the Rhayader and Elan walks together by the delightful 3 miles (each way) walk along the tarmac path following the old railway line.

Terrain: hilly, and likely to be muddy in many places.

Maps:O.S. Landranger 147 or Explorer 200

Starting points: GR971682 in the main car park in Rhayader, and GR928647 in the parking area at the Elan Visitor Centre. Getting there is along the A44 from Leominster or A 470 from Builth Wells or Llangurig.

Public Transport: there are bus links with Llandrindod Wells.

Facilities: Tourist Information Centres in Rhayader (01597 810591) and Elan Valley (closed in mid-winter), and choice of refreshments in Rhayader.

Weather

Generally a wet and windy month, though often quite mild, this year it turned out to be a fairly dry month, and the driest November since 1988. It was sunnier than average and 2°C above average too, with most days exceeding 10°C, the average daytime maximum for the month. Fogs and frosts were scarce but there were a few very wet and windy days. The rainy start to the month produced floods in the first week, but then the pressure rose to give an anticyclonic second week, with cooler north-westerly weather. North-westerly airstreams have been more frequent in recent years, and they contribute to slightly higher sunshine totals than in former decades. Cold northerlies around the 20th gave day maxima of only 6°C and light snow showers were seen in the Welsh Borders. This cold spell was not exceptional, when compared with cold snaps in previous

Novembers. Complete snow covers were experienced in November 1996 and 1993.

Ice in November brings mud in December, is fairly reliable old saying as both types of weather are likely to be experienced sometime in both months. From the 22nd onwards, mild and windy weather was experienced, with stormy winds around the 25th, and nearly all the leaves had fallen by the end of the month. The largely frost free conditions enabled lawns to keep growing throughout most of the month.

The Countryside

Together with September and October, this month makes up autumn and this has been the sunniest autumn of the last 40 years. We generally regard the end of the autumn as nearly the end of the year, but in Celtic times it was seen as the start of the year. The animals were brought indoors in preparation for the winter, and plans were formulated for the next year of farming. Farmers nowadays are not as numerous and are probably still filling in forms for the past year as well as looking ahead, probably with limited optimism. Moving west from the undulating lowlands of Herefordshire, and into the Welsh Hill country around Rhayader, notice the brown colour on the hills (both grass and bracken) and the greens of the lowlands. The lowland landscape is mainly green fields, with hedges as field boundaries. Although many of these are cut back severely, many old traditional hedges in this area are dense and of double thickness, which is very good for wild life. There are still a few animals to be seen in the fields, mainly sheep, which often look like white dots on the hillsides. There are a few cattle around in the valley, where grazing is still quite good this year. In addition to the grass, the valley has a few stubble fields and fields where tractors are hard at work, ploughing in preparation for planting winter crops. They are generally accompanied by gulls, which drift up the river in their search for food. Birds are mostly quiet, though the gulls, as well as rooks, jackdaws and starlings are never silent, and flocks of the shy fieldfares make big noises as they fly away. Buzzards are often to be seen floating overhead, as is true in much of the Wye Valley, but in this area are the much larger red kites, the **bird of the month**. With

Red kite

a wing span of about 6 feet the red kite is a marvellous flier and easily recognised by its forked tail. This bird has staged a marvellous recovery from near extinction in Britain and with considerable help from man is now thriving in a few parts of Mid Wales as well as in the Chilterns and other selected areas. They feed on carrion, small mammals and occasionally birds, as well as worms and insects.

A few leaves survive on some of the trees, mainly the oak near the end of the month, but the reds and yellows of autumn, which survived until early November, have gone by the end of the month.

November's sky is chill and drear
November's leaf is red and sear
(Sir Walter Scott in *Marmion*).

Most coniferous trees retain their green colour, though it is dark at this time of year. Where the deciduous larch trees have shed their needles, a brownish-golden colour on the trees and the ground, adds to the scenic value of these woods. Many of the woods in this area are man-made, and managed (by Forest Enterprise) and lakes too have been created by man. Are they not improvements to this landscape?

Elan Valley

The Elan Valley Visitor Centre (01597 810898) is open from early March until the end of October, and contains information, an exhibition, café and toilets. In the car park and picnic area is a sculpture to Percy Bysshe Shelley, inspired by Prometheus Unbound. In the centre, Shelley is in deep creative thought and alongside him are female dancing nymph-like figures, representing Muses. His link with this area is that he came to live here for a time, with his 16 year old wife, after being expelled from Oxford for atheism.

Rainfall is heavy in this area, averaging 1800mm per annum, hence the turbulent streams, waterfalls and large reservoirs. Water is one of the main exports from Wales as the weather systems from the Atlantic drop much of their moisture when they hit the Welsh hills. Hydroelectric power is generated from the base of all the dams and also from the Foel Tower. An Information Board at the entrance to the Visitor Centre Car Park tells us that the Elan Estate is owned by Welsh Water. The catchments of the Elan and Claerwen cover 70 square miles of rugged Welsh countryside in which four of the dams and reservoirs were built between 1892-1904, supplying Birmingham with water since 1904. The fifth dam, Claerwen, was built later, 1946-52, by when it was realised that the demand for water could not be met by the existing schemes. In the past, mining was important, even as long ago as Roman times, and still had some importance for lead, copper and other minerals in the 19th century. Sheep farming has been important for centuries, together with some quarrying.

Rhayader

Often described as the Gateway to Wild Wales, the town's name is derived from Rhaeadr Gwy, the waterfall on the Wye. This old market town, with a population of 2000, is close to the Elan Valley and has road links with all the neighbouring towns. It is home to the Welsh Royal Crystal company, and although its old tannery industry has disappeared, wool and pottery have both been revived here. The livestock market is situated close to the church and the Leisure Centre. The church of St Clement was largely rebuilt in 1733 and the present church dates from 1887. There was a castle in Rhayader, not dating from Norman times, but built in the 12th century by the Welsh Prince, Rhys ap Grufydd. Rhayader also achieved fame in the past as the location of some of the Rebecca riots, when the local people objected to the toll charges on the roads, and the men dressed up as women to attack the turnpike gates. The name is thought to have been derived from the quote in Genesis, which says that Rebecca's descendants *will possess the gates of them that hate them.*

Gigrin Farm

Located half a mile south of Rhayader on the A470, this farm feeds the red kites at 2 pm daily, and also offers Bed and Breakfast and self catering accommodation, as well as a camping and caravan site. The fields surrounding the 350 year old farmhouse are mainly used for rearing sheep. A nature trail has been created around the fields and on the hillside, and special hides have been built adjacent to the field where the kites are fed. At this feeding station, 50 or more kites may be seen, as well as buzzards, ravens, crows and magpies.

Riverside Walk

The clock tower memorial in Rhayader

From the car park adjacent to the Information Centre, walk to the cross roads and the War Memorial Clock Tower (1), built in 1923. If visiting Gigrin Farm for the 2 pm feeding, walk along the Builth Road A470 for just over a quarter mile. On the right you will notice the sign for the Riverside Path, which is our route after visiting Gigrin, which is a few metres further along the road, on the left, passing the Brynafon House Country Hotel, formerly the workhouse.

After seeing the kite feeding, there is the option of walking the Nature Trail around the farm and then retracing steps to the riverside path and walking back to Rhayader alongside the Wye. An Information Board on the riverside path mentions kingfisher, dipper, grey wagtail, goosander and Common sandpiper, so keep looking in the hope of seeing interesting birds – although sandpiper will only be here in the summer. There are occasional picnic tables alongside the path, and just before reaching the buildings of Rhayader we pass the rugby ground on our right. Walk up Water Lane to reach the main road (2).

If not going to Gigrin, turn right at the Town Clock (1) and walk along West Street to reach Water Lane (2). Keep straight ahead to cross the bridge over the River Wye, noting the falls to the left, then turn left along the narrow road signed to Gro Park and Wye Valley Walk, for a walk of 3 miles.

Pass the church on the right, and the park and football pitch on the left and follow the narrow road. It bends right, where a Private track leads left to Ddole Farm, and then climbs up steeply away from the town. Pass New House on the left, with its large barn and soon reach a left bend, where a stony track goes straight ahead (3). The track is the route of our return along the Wye Valley Walk, and looking along it gives views into the Elan Valley, but we just continue along the road. Walking along this lane might reveal views overhead of buzzards or kites, which are quite numerous in this area.

The road descends and we enter the woods, passing a bridleway coming from the left, from Ddole Farm. The wood ends on the left and the River Wye and main road are down to the left. Shortly the wood ends on the right, and we turn here, along the track, signed Wye Valley Walk. There are old lichen-encrusted oaks in the wood to our right, and open fields to the left. Where the track bends right, an embankment of the old railway line is on our left. We reach a gate, and a junction of tracks, but go right-left to keep straight ahead, and pass between barns to soon reach a T-junction (4) of tracks, where we have a choice of routes. The left turn leads to the barns and buildings of Glan Elan, the right turn is the Wye Valley Way, but straight ahead is perhaps the best choice here.

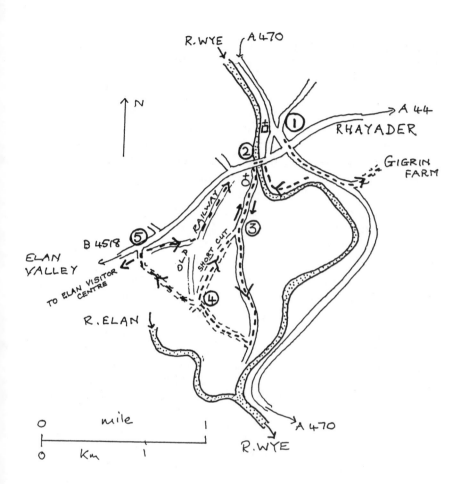

Short Cut

For the shortest route back to Rhayader, turn right along the stony track between hedges and follow this lane to reach the narrow road **(3)** where we walked earlier. Retrace steps back into Rhayader, enjoying the views over the town to the surrounding hills as we descend the hill. At the main road, turn right to pass the United Reform Church and the Old Police Station (now an Antiques Centre) to reach the shops and the Town Clock again.

Main Route

Just slightly left of straight ahead is a bridleway, through a metal gate and along a track between hedges. The route of the old railway line is now on our right. We pass the edge of a wood on the left, and keep straight ahead, staying close to the right side of a fairly large field, which narrows near the end. Go through the metal gate and on to a track, passing a small house on the right, a larger house (Neuadd) on the left and then the large buildings of Noyadd Farm. Just before reaching the road (B4518) linking Rhayader with the Elan Valley, we can see the cross path of the surfaced Elan Valley Trail **(5)**. A left turn here will give a delightful 3 mile extension to the Elan Valley Visitor Centre, staying between the road and the Elan River. In autumn colours or indeed at any time of the year, this is a gorgeous walk through fabulous scenery, and provides a link with the Caban Coch and Elan walk (described later) if required.

Turn right along the trail if returning to Rhayader, following the route of the old railway line. Cross over an old bridge and admire the wonderful views all around and the modernised house and barn up to the left. We reach the former railway junction, where we are joined from the right by the route of the Mid Wales Valley line, part of the Cambrian railway, and the combined route goes through the gate on our left towards Rhayader. Notice the numerous trees alongside the route – not leaves on the line nowadays, but leaves on the footpath in the autumn.

Our path begins to climb and the cutting and end of the tunnel can be seen down to our left. We pass piles of scree and former diggings and beyond a cross track reach an open grassy area, rich in flowers and butterflies. An Information Board tells us that this is a Nature Reserve, purchased in 1992 with a Donation from the Vincent Wildlife Trust and is looked after by the Radnorshire Wildlife Trust, and has obtained money from the Heritage Lottery fund. The reason for this location becoming a Nature Reserve is the importance of the tunnel as a roost for bats, including the uncommon Daubenton's and Natterers. There is no public access to the tunnel.

As we begin to descend we pass the bottom end of the tunnel, and the cutting down to our right, then pass through two new gates and across the line of the old railway. Carry on descending slightly, with old railway to our left, and views of Rhayader on our right.

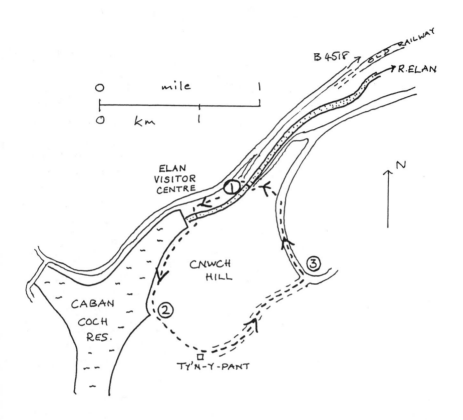

We reach the Information Board for the Elan Valley Trail, which follows the route of the old Birmingham Corporation Railway built in the 1890s to help work in the construction of the dams. It was a standard gauge railway and had links with the Cambrian Railway. The trail follows the route for 8 miles from Cwmdauddwr to Craig Goch dam and Pen y Garreg reservoir and is for cyclists and horseriders as well as walkers.

Go through the gateway, with carvings by the artist Reece Ingram, and turn right to reach the first houses. Pass the Rhayader Information Board on our right, near the small car park, the Triangle Inn, the Parish Pound and St Bride's church. The road to Gro Park is next on our right and we walk on across the river bridge and back into the town.

Caban Coch and Elan Walk

Pass to the right of the Visitor Centre **(1)**, towards Caban Coch dam (37m – 120ft high), and walk on beyond the Children's Playground area to the right of the Turbine House, with its small hydro electricity turbine. Then turn left to cross the bridge and round the right side

The Caban Coch dam

of the other Turbine House to the steep steps up through the rhododendrons, interspersed with a few hawthorn and rowan, and a patch of heather. The path is partially stepped but partly slippery stones. At the top of this climb pass through

the gate, to the top of the dam and good views up and down the valley. Walk along the side of the reservoir across the picnic area and follow the stony path, which leads to some steps, for the Elan Woodland Walk. After gaining some height, we follow the fairly level path through bracken, heather and whinberry. Fork left to go up again, following the yellow arrow and the Elan Woodland Walk sign. Passing through ancient oak woodland, the path begins to turn left into a narrow tributary valley, and soon divides, where we take the left fork **(2)** and begin a steep climb.

Look back at the good views up the reservoir, to the bridge, which separates Caban Coch reservoir from Garreg Ddu. Just to the left of the bridge is Nantgwyllt church built in 1903 as the Chapel of Ease for the parish of Cwmdeuddwr, to replace the old church flooded by the reservoir. Also flooded was Nantgwyllt House, where the Shelleys lived for a time, and possibly provided the inspiration for Francis Brett Young's novel, "The House under the Water". We soon pass an old building to our right, which was Nant-y-Gro dam, where explosives for the Dambusters raids in World War II were tested.

Go on beyond the coniferous woodland on our right and out into the open bracken-covered hillside. At the top is another patch of conifers and where the path divides (right for the Woodland Walk) we fork left, with fir trees on our right. Just beyond these trees, the ruin of the old house, Ty'n-y-Pant (meaning 'the house in the hollow') is to our right, and we are climbing gently through bracken to reach the top of the hill, and two posts with horseshoe signs. At a height of 400 metres (1300ft), pass the line of concrete posts marking the edge of the Elan Estate, and begin our descent along a stony track. Wide views open out all around as we descend steeply to a gate, beyond which is an RSPB sign.

Walk on down the surfaced lane, which we descend steeply and after half a mile reach a T-junction, and turn left (3). Walk along this narrow road for half a mile or so, with woodland on our right and open land and Cnwch Hill to our left. Just beyond the drive to the farm complex, Cnwch Farm, look for path to the left, which we take as it leads down through the grass and bracken. Just beyond a marker post, with a blue spot, buildings can be seen ahead, and the path splits. We go left here, steeply down through heather and small silver birch trees to cross the stream and reach the small wooden gate. The buildings of Elan Village built in 1909, and including a chapel and a school, can be clearly seen to our right, as we follow a fairly level path, but when this splits we fork left alongside the wire fence, and descend to a stile and an Information Board, where we turn right to cross the bridge over the River Elan, and turn left back to the Visitor Centre.

The Information Board is at the beginning of the Cnwch Wood Nature Trail and it is well worth following this path if you feel energetic and have enough time. One hour should be ample to follow the half-mile trail which zigzags up to the top of the wood, passing several information boards on the way. The wood is an SSSI and is noted for its oak trees, wild flowers, lichens and rich bird life, which includes pied flycatcher and redstart in the summer.

December
Chepstow

There is a choice of two walks from Chepstow, one going through woods on the valley side, following the Wye Valley Walk and returning across Piercefield Park and alongside the race course, and the other going downstream to see where the Wye reaches the estuary of the River Severn and the sea, and also find the beginning of the Offa's Dyke Path on top of the Sedbury cliffs overlooking the Severn estuary. Walking through woods will give shelter, which may be appreciated at this time of year, but the open stretch in Piercefield Park and even more open top of Sedbury Cliffs will be more exhilarating.

Lengths of walks: The walk to Piercefield is about 6 miles and the other walk to the Offa's Stone and back is about 7 miles. Obviously the two could be joined together to give a day's walk of about 13 miles, requiring about 6 hours.

Terrain: undulating and occasionally steep when on the valley side, and the ground is likely to be very muddy at this time of year, unless frozen hard.

Map: O.S. Outdoor Leisure 14, Wye Valley and Forest of Dean, or Landranger 162.

Starting point: the car park alongside Chepstow castle, GR535942. This is reached along the M4 and M48, the A48 from Gloucester or the A466 from Monmouth.

Facilities: Chepstow has a main line station and has bus links with Monmouth, Newport, Bristol and Gloucester. There is a Tourist Information Centre in Chepstow, open throughout the year (telephone number 01291 623772). A choice of refreshments is available in Chepstow, and also a pub near the route through Sedbury.

Weather

A changeable month, usual for December, was mainly mild and windy, with a series of low pressure systems crossing from west to east. They were quite active, bringing heavy rain as well as strong winds, but moved quickly to give sunny periods in between the depressions to cause the sunniest December since 1962. The first week of the month was mild and wet, with day temperatures up to 13°C, and this coincided with one of Buchan's warm spells (from 3rd until 14th). The wind turned northerly for a few days to give lower temperatures, and snow on the 18th was followed by the only cold snap of the month. High pressure dominated for a few days from the 20th, and minus 8°C was recorded in many places, including the Wye Valley, and several inches of snow covered large areas, even in the lowlands. Milder weather took over again in time for Christmas and the month ended with mild and wet weather. The Meteorological Office records that the final week of the year is frequently a stormy period. Most of the country was green, but in London a few flakes of snow were seen on the roof of the Weather Centre and so it was classified as a White Christmas for those who had been betting. White Christmases are quite rare, though Victorians remembered them as being frequent, possibly because Dickens wrote about them as through they were a regular occurrence. He was born in 1812, and there were six white Christmases in his first nine years.

The Countryside

A green Christmas makes a fat churchyard is an ancient piece of folk lore based on the assumption that frosty weather kills off the germs and is therefore healthier. If true, this may be another subject to be assessed with the effects of global warming.

'*At Christmas meadows green, at Easter covered with frost.*' This supposed link between Christmas and Easter weather has no sound basis at all, as there is no connection between weather conditions so many months apart. In recent years, however, there have been more snow showers over the Easter period than at the preceding Christmas.

Rain or frost seem to be the most likely alternatives for winter walkers to experience, although we always hope for one of those rare bright sunny days. Mud is very likely, which is why country dwellers make good use of wellington boots – though not recommended for walkers. This is apparently a dead time of year, but there is plenty of life beneath the ground as the daffodil bulbs are beginning to show through, and farm fields have spring crops that have already sprouted an inch or two. The bare trees reveal their magnificent shapes, with thousands of tiny branches, making wonderful silhouettes, portrayed by many artists. Mistletoe stands out clearly in some old orchards, and along a few avenues of trees, as it is still common in parts of the Wye Valley, although decreasing in most locations. In addition to the traditional mistle thrushes, it is now spread by black-caps, which are more frequently staying in Britain for the winter. The green leaves of holly add colour to the scenery, and with bright red berries too if not already eaten by the birds. Other colour is provided by the first hazel catkins, some yellow gorse and this is a good time of year to look carefully at the patterns and shapes in the moss and lichens. The presence of lichens is an indication of little or no pollution, and some trees and walls have good growth of lichen facing in one direction, but nothing on the other side. Several varieties of lichen are quite shrubby, but others are merely leafy or flat along the rocks or trees. Amongst the birds likely to be seen on this walk are the gulls, particularly two varieties from this large group, though not the misleadingly named common gull, as it is not very common. Much more numerous are the **birds of the month,** the black headed gull with its red legs and beak, and a dark brown head in summer but only a couple of black spots in winter; and the larger herring gull with its greyish back, flesh coloured legs and feet and a vicious looking yellow beak with a red spot. These birds may be seen on the river, or sitting on the mud or on the parapet of the bridge, or just floating lazily and effortlessly overhead – occasionally joined in this leisurely activity by a buzzard.

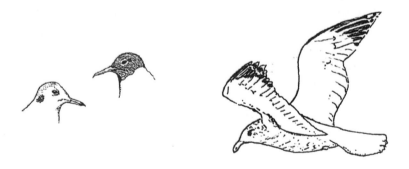

Left: **black-headed gull in (far left) winter and summer plumage.**
Right: herring gull

Offa's Dyke

This famous boundary is mainly marked by an earthwork, but south of Monmouth the River Wye was considered to be an adequate boundary. King Offa conquered most of England south of the Humber, but his most famous memorial is this earthwork, stretching from Sedbury Cliffs overlooking the Severn Estuary to the north Wales coast at Prestatyn, a distance of nearly 150 miles – what a task! This was the boundary between his (Saxon) territory and the Ancient Britons to the west. Offa's Dyke Path is mentioned in the Introduction (page 2).

Chepstow

Situated at a crossing point of the River Wye, Chepstow has been an important centre since Roman times, and much of its history can be seen in the museum located in a late 18th-century town house on Bridge Street down by the river. Near this house is the graceful bridge which dates from 1816, a little upstream from the newer and higher bridge, opened in 1988 to enable traffic to bypass the narrow and winding streets of this old town. Remnants of the 13th-century wall can be seen in the town, as well as the old gateway, which had a gate and guardroom, and was used for collecting tolls, until the 19th century. Dominating the river edge is the impressive Norman castle standing on the limestone cliffs, and another prominent building is the church of St Mary, founded in 1071. The nave is all that remains from the Benedictine priory founded by William Fitz Osbern at that time. It had links with Cormeilles in Normandy, which recently has been relinked with Chepstow as a twin town. Chepstow was a port and industrial town, though the industries declined at the time of the Industrial Revolution. Edward Davies, writing in the 18th century said:

> *Corn, cider, timber are exported hence,*
> *And ships are built for traffic and defence:*
> *The Irish trade increases ev'ry day,*
> *And ships from Chepstow visit Dublin Bay.*

Chepstow became a market town in 1294 and was a port from Norman times until the mid-19th century. The greatest prosperity of the 18th and 19th centuries is shown by several of the buildings surviving from that time.

Chepstow Castle

Situated on top of the limestone cliff overlooking the Wye, this was the first stone castle to be built in Wales. Parts of the cellars and lower storeys of the tower survive from the original castle begun by William Fitz Osbern in 1067, on behalf of William the Conqueror. Additions were made to the castle by later owners, and the present day castle is an amalgam of different periods. The name of Henry Marten is remembered in the tower where he was kept prisoner for 20 years, after being one of those who signed the death warrant of Charles I. In a good state of repair, the present day castle was owned by the Clare family in the 12th century, then by William Marshal, Earl of Pembroke who made several additions to it in about 1200. Subsequently, Roger Bigod, Earl of Norfolk improved the accommodation between 1270 and 1300, and was responsible for building the town wall and gate.

Chepstow Castle

Walking upstream

From the car park **(1)** by the TIC, Castle View Hotel and the castle itself, walk along the left side of the castle, following the Wye Valley Walk signpost. This leads us up a dry valley known as The Dell, and provides good views of the huge walls and stone work in the castle, probably with noisy jackdaws flying above the tall walls. Climb steeply up, passing a stone seat for four people to sit and have conversations. Go on beyond the castle, to emerge at the road, where we turn right, and proceed steadily uphill. Pass a primary school and near the top of the hill, at the Wye Valley signpost **(2)**, turn right into the parking area for the school and leisure centre. At the far left corner of the car park, the path goes on between fences, with the school on the left and woods on the right. Notice the reddish stems of dogwood bushes over to the left.

At the end of the school grounds, go through a gap in the wall, and turn right, down a few steps and follow the path to reach a fine viewpoint with a handrail, and a seat. Look back to the castle and new road bridge in Chepstow, and on towards the Severn Estuary and the Severn Bridge.

The woods are mainly deciduous and bare at this time of year. A few birds may be heard and seen, and grey squirrels are quite numerous. Not much is growing, but there are patches of ferns, including areas where hart's tongue thrives. We follow the winding path through the woods, passing a narrow path going off left, and then climbing again, the path bends right with hart's tongue fern to our left. In an area of laurel, pass a small grotto on the left, one of many features created by Valentine Morris the owner of the Piercefield Estate in the mid-18th century. He also laid out the path and many other walks around his estate. The river can be seen very steeply down to our right, and across on the other bank, looking northwards to the middle of the lowland area, is the small settlement of Lancaut, with the remains of the abandoned Norman church of St James.

Continuing along the fairly level path now, we begin to swing round right, following the curve of the river meander, and must be on the look out for a small path going off diagonally to the left **(3)**, where an open field can just be seen through the trees. This is the route of our onward walk, but first continue along the Wye Valley path for just over half a mile, ignoring the path going left up some steps, and then reach the Giant's Cave. This is a hollow through a large rock, and the Wye Valley path goes straight on through here. The path here is perched on the side of a very steep slope, and views to the river are quite grand at this time of year, when it is possible to see through the trees.

At this point, retrace steps for the half mile (10-15 minutes) to reach our onward path (3), which climbs up through the trees for a few metres, to reach a stile on the edge of the woods. Go over here, and follow the line of fence on the right, to walk past the ruins of Piercefield House. Valentine Morris owned the house in the 18th century and it was he who created paths in the woods, and opened the park to the public. George Smith, the owner from 1784-94, extended the house and built the stables, then Sir Mark Wood (1794-1802) rebuilt much of the house and added the two wings that can still be seen today. There were other owners before it was sold to the Racecourse Company. Racing began here in 1929.

We pass in front of the house and, when the fence ends, keep straight ahead to the left of a clump of trees. Note the grand views out to the left, and the old buildings including the stable block to the right. Beyond the trees, join a stony track leading across the park, with the Race Course to the right.

Leave the park at a cattle grid, and follow the track through woods. A large wall will soon be noticed on the left, and when the track bends sharp right, go left along the path which stays close to the wall, and follow this through the trees to reach the road through a gap in the wall. Turn left, and follow this road as it leads back into Chepstow.

The walk downstream to Sedbury Cliffs and Offa's Dyke

From the car park (1) walk past the TIC and along the road to the bridge, looking out for sandbags by the doorways, evidence of recent flood danger. Pass the Bridge Hotel and go on to the graceful bridge, one of many on this site, and look to see if the tide is in, and try to recognise any gulls which are floating or sitting around here. The tidal range at the bridge is up to 14m (46ft) maximum, the second highest in the world (after the Bay of Fundy)

Cross over the bridge to enter Gloucestershire and England, and as the road bends left, go straight ahead and up a paved lane, following signs for the Gloucestershire Way. Halfway up the hill (4), turn right along another surfaced lane, still climbing, between walls and houses. This is now the Offa's Dyke path and as the lane levels, we take a narrow path going off downhill to the right, and providing

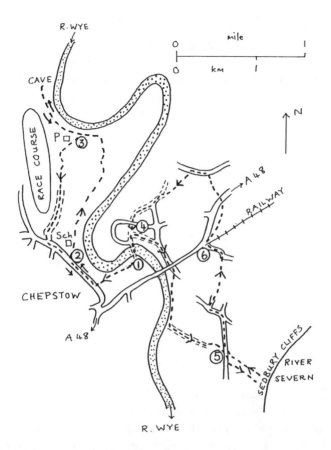

views over the river to a small industrial zone in Chepstow. Our path climbs up a few steps to pass some new houses and on to a narrow road, lined with the first signs of daffodils and winter heliotrope (a garden escapee). Reach a road where we turn right, and walk over the bridge above road and railway. Notice the railway tunnel to the left (we shall pass the far end of this later) and to the right is the railway bridge built in 1852 by Brunel, as was the station in Chepstow.

Take the first right turn after the bridge, Wye Bank Avenue, and turn left at the T-junction, then after a few more metres, go right along a narrow footpath between fence and hedge, following the signpost to Sedbury Cliff. We skirt round the edge of urban development of Sedbury for the next mile or so. The path is following the line of the river, with views to old works on the other side of the river. Emerge to a patch of grass, with bungalows over to the left, and trees on our right, staying close to the fence. As the road bends away left, we go right along a narrow path passing more bungalows, to emerge to an open patch, with views of the Severn Bridge ahead. Reach a stony track, where we turn left, to pass a Sewage Works on our right.

The Severn Bridge

Come along to houses, but keep straight ahead as far as the point where the road goes right, and we turn left to follow the footpath sign along a narrow path. When this reaches another road, Norse Way, turn right, to walk down to a footbridge, cross a track and over a stile into a field. Go up to the top of the field and in the corner is a stile, beyond which is the road (5). Go right for 20-30 metres, and then left along the Private Road with a footpath sign. At the end of this road, go right over the stile and then left to follow the field boundary. This leads down to the corner and another stile, and keep straight ahead to the stile at the end of the next field to reach the grassy flood plain on the edge of the Severn Estuary, which is very wide at high tide.

Our route is a few metres left, to another stile, but first have a walk ahead, to look at the river, and the Severn Bridge. The wooden structure seen 200-300 metres downstream is the framework of an old salmon putcher, used in former years when large numbers of salmon were caught as they came upstream. There are likely to be birds around here, such as the bright sheld duck, as well as gulls and perhaps cormorants. Notice the Sedbury Cliffs on this side of the river, a popular location for geologists, though perhaps not as famous as the Aust cliffs on the far bank, by the Severn Bridge. The cliffs consist of rocks from the Keuper period, with red clays at the bottom and Tea Green Marls higher up. Above these is a narrow band of Rhaetic beds, noted for the fossil remains such as Ichtyosaurs and Plesiosaurs as found at Aust, and at the top of the cliffs are thin bands of limestone of the Lower Liassic period. Erosion ensures that all types of rocks, often containing fossils, fall down on to the flood plain. Dating from more modern times is Oldbury Power Station, seen upstream across the river.

For the final hundred metres to the beginning of Offa's Dyke long-distance footpath, go over the stile away from the river, but do not go straight ahead along the track by the hedge on the left. Instead, turn right, with fence on your right and climb steeply up to get to the top of Sedbury Cliffs, At the top of this ascent is the stone which marks the beginning (or end) of Offa's Dyke path, which is a long-distance route stretching for 176 miles to Prestatyn on the coast of North Wales. I walked this route many years ago, with my elder daughter, and it passes through glorious scenery all the way, but beware of the stiles as we counted more than 670 on the route.

Turn left at the stone and descend steeply to a small footbridge, and then up the other side along an embankment which is part of the original dyke. The path levels off and we go over a stile and on to a black kissing gate, then left to the road **(5)**. Here we turn right, to follow the road as it leads into Sedbury, passing an old iron milestone (Chepstow 2 miles). Continue along the road as it bends left, up into Sedbury, and at the top of the slope is a Post Office on the right just beyond which (and before reaching the pub on the left) we turn right along a road between houses. When this road bends right, go straight ahead on to a path passing alongside some old buildings, houses and small industries on the left, with fields to the right. The path becomes straight for about 300 metres before bending left to pass round old farm buildings. We emerge on to a road opposite a restored stone building and turn left to follow this narrow road to where it crosses over the railway, but then ends because of the modern major road. To the left is the railway tunnel (we passed the opposite end of this tunnel earlier), and to the right there is the relic of an old branch line which used to extend northwards into the Wye Valley to Tintern and beyond.

Once over the railway we go right **(6)**, through a gate and into the field, staying close to the right side of two fields before swinging round left to the far corner of the second field to reach the road. When I last walked there, the path was not available as the farmer had used the full width of the field to the hedge, and so it may be necessary to walk along the right margin of these two fields. Go straight over the road (A48), taking care as it is busy with fast moving traffic, and go over a stile by the clump of trees. Proceed along the left margin of a large field, then over a stile and straight ahead to cross a smaller field, heading to the right of the house ahead. Then go over three stiles to cross two small paddocks and reach a narrow road, where we turn left. Walk past The Willows and a few other houses of Old Bishton, passing some fine old stone walls, and a modern tennis court on the right. Just beyond these houses, where a path comes in from the right to cross the road, we turn left, as this is the Gloucestershire Way, which we follow back into Chepstow.

Go left through a large gate, and head down across the middle of the field towards a large gate. Up to the right can be seen a small church and school. Pass through an iron kissing gate by the large iron gate, and alongside a fence with a patch of horticulture to the left. There is delightful countryside around here, with views over the estuary. At the end of this field, go over a stone slab stile and along a narrow path between fence and hedge. This leads through to a small road where we turn right for a few metres and then left along the larger road. When this road splits, by the Tidenham War Memorial Hall, take the right fork (Mopla Road) the Cycle Route to Chepstow. Offa's Dyke Path comes in from the right, to join us, and we continue between hedges, gradually downhill to reach a road, which we cross. Go straight ahead descending ever more steeply down a surfaced lane leading to the point where we turned a couple of hours ago **(4)**. We just keep straight ahead downhill to reach the road and the river bridge, beyond which is our starting point and more important now, our finishing point too.